The Adverse Effects of Leftist Social Policy

Conspicuous Compassion, Cultural
Corrosion, and Collectivism

RICHARD MERLO

LifeRich Publishing is a registered trademark of The Reader's Digest Association, Inc.

LifeRich Publishing books may be ordered through booksellers or by contacting:

LifeRich Publishing
1663 Liberty Drive
Bloomington, IN 47403
www.liferichpublishing.com
1 (888) 238-8637

ISBN: 978-1-4897-1994-2 (sc)
ISBN: 978-1-4897-1995-9 (e)

Print information available on the last page.

LifeRich Publishing rev. date: 11/05/2018

Contents

Introduction

The United States is on the verge of exchanging its traditional capitalist order for socialism. Many leftist-Democrat votes will be needed to establish the new order, and, to that end, an underclass dependent on the US welfare state is being created and collected. Under the guise of "compassion," the immigration of large numbers of refugees (Mexican, Central American, and Middle Eastern) is encouraged, by illegal entry if necessary. Mexican radio broadcasts have coached many of these illegals so that they enter understanding how best to approach the border bureaucracy, how to remain in the country despite improper documentation, and how to receive the many welfare benefits available. Democrats hurry to be the first to extend their welcome, to explain how handouts will be distributed, and to make sure the immigrant understands the quid pro quo: "When you're able to vote, it must be for the Democrats."

'Since 2005, more than nine million foreign nationals have arrived in the US by chain migration, and when they become voting citizens, in all likelihood, two-thirds of them will vote democrat' (1)

The needs of an enlarging dependent underclass will be met by America's welfare state, and leftist Democrats will ensure their reelections by commiting to an egalitarian, redistributionist policy, which looks increasingly socialist. Inverting JFK's inaugural advice (11), his party now asks what their country can do for this underclass. The Left will explain to US citizens that this generosity is needed to lessen the gap between rich and poor, and those of us who protest will be called racist, xenophobic white supremacists. Compassion, they will insist, requires us to admit even those with no skills and little ability. Inevitably, criminals and terrorists will slip through at San Ysidro, but their number will be small, we are assured, and (we are delighted to hear) in no greater proportion than America's native criminal class. America already has many native rapists and murderers, but we are urged to import even more.

These new immigrants will form part of an enlarging dependent subculture voting reliably Democratic. Americans will gradually be persuaded by the Left that it only makes sense to issue them drivers' licenses (to make them "more accountable") and, after a decent interval, those licenses will be used to register them to vote. The Left expects American taxpayers to subsidize these illegals, who are described as "disadvantaged" victims of the capitalist order, which enshrines greed and excessive competition. To display our commitment to "social justice,", and compassion, and to atone for black America's past and ongoing oppression by whites, we must share our wealth with these illegals. Sharing is meant to dispel any memory of slavery, Jim Crow, oppression of non-whites, and "otherism." Dividing and redistributing will require higher taxes. Expropriation of the very affluent may be needed, but the Left will call that "taxation" as well. This will bring us even further on the path to collective statism. Socialism will be expensive, but the Left will use rich people's money until(as Mrs. Thatcher cautioned) it runs out.

Not too many years ago, the French government raised the marginal income tax rate above 70 percent, which prompted the departure of many rich Parisians to London, making it the second wealthiest French city. We've seen the beginning of "capital flight" in the United States (Burger King to Canada, Pfizer to Ireland), and the Left risks more capital departing the country if taxation is overly punitive. But they are gambling that enough capital will remain to be distributed to its voters and finance the quiet revolution.

And the US voter, superficially educated and ignorant of socialism's many failures, is vulnerable to leftist demagoguery. Promises of free medical care, education, food, housing, and so on convince many to support leftist politicians, not understanding that (a) the capitalist order is the source of their material wealth, (b) countries with a socialist order are inevitably poorer, and (c) the two systems are mutually exclusive, so that a socialist order with capitalist production is a contradiction in terms. But liberal-socialist promises are seductive:

"Many … millennials … seem to want the financial security of childhood without the baggage of parents and expect Washington to fill the void." (2)

But the political left is gambling once again, hoping that by the time the voters understand socialism's disadvantages, it will be too late to turn back. In the meantime, subversion of all kinds will be created and exploited to expedite capitalism's demise. It will beginsubtly, perhaps publishing the income-figures of wealthy industrialists; gradually, our founding myths will be undermined (Thomas Jefferson, we are told, dallied with Sally Hemmings; and everybody who signed the Declaration was a white oppressor) Our minority communities will be told repeatedly how whites have cheated them. Rioting and violent crime will follow, while leftist academe will permit arson, and student anarchy. An enormous welfare state will end in national bankruptcy, which will be explained as inevitable under the capitalist order. But we'll be reassured that all will be well in the new socialist state, which will include 'globalization', in which the United States will lose its national status, perhaps to become simply a province in a much larger world government, like the European Union. Erlers sees the disadvantages of this plan:

'Historically, constitutional government…(and its protection of the individual citizen)…has been found only in the nation-state. Where the people share a common good and are dedicated to the same principles and purposes. The homogenous world-state… (which Liberal Leftism promotes)…-the European union on a global scale—will not be a constitutional democracy. It will be the administration of 'universal personhood' without the inconvenience of having to rely on the consent of the governed. It will be government by unelected and unaccountable bureaucrats…like the burgeoning administrative state…expanding its reach…and power…in the United States.' (1)

I A

Who are the Left? An Attempt at Definition

In 1789, the French king was going broke. Trying to raise cash, he convened a congress—the Estates General. Seating was arranged according to political inclination: those who favored the retention of the monarchy sat to the right of the presiding officer, and those hoping for radical governmental change sat to his left. Hence the terms "right" and "left." This is a cautionary tale, and it could be a metaphor for the capitalist order in America, because by activating the French Left, Louis XVI unwittingly arranged his own beheading.

The Left, for our purposes, refers to those wanting radical sociocultural, political change; to include those wishing for minor change would make the definition overbroad, and so those moderates are excluded. The term *leftism*, as used here, is more or less synonymous with socialism, statism, collectivism, progressivism, and liberalism. More recently, the Leftist wing of the US Democratic Party has admitted its commitment to socialism. Simply put, the Democratic Left wants to replace capitalism with socialism, and are counting on the revenge of 'disadvantaged' voters for their 'oppression' by 'greedy capitalists'.

'Socialism combines imperfect understanding of human cooperation with the ne'er-do-well's resentment…many are filled with resentment and rage when they think of fortunate speculators… Noone shall be rich if I am poor…' (3)

'One of our two political parties is being swept by a young and rising new left that is fiercely progressive and on fire for Socialism. It may in coming decades sweep the … corporations away, if they cannot rouse themselves.' (4)

'I think the alt-left folks are working toward now … chaos, anarchy, and regime overthrow … and we should be alert to their intentions.' (5)

'[Lenin] continued to sanction the secret dispatch of money, spies and propaganda to the rest of the world … He did what he could to divide the capitalist powers among themselves. He did not explain how the balance would be kept between a rapprochement with such powers and an enhancement of the Interests of global Socialist revolution'. (6)

The following groups are often or always leftist in the United States:

1. Socialist ideologues
2. Liberal intellectuals, often academics
3. Journalists and entertainers
4. Liberals, often conspicuously compassionate, in our own neighborhoods

Like some diseases, the US Left is sometimes dormant. Keeping a low profile, it awaits social instability, perhaps an economic crisis or an unpopular war, to reactivate. During the Great Depression, it became clear that there was a political fifth column in the United States. Large immigrations from Eastern and Southern Europe in the late nineteenth and early twentieth century included Italian Anarchists and Russian Communists. These began to subvert American capitalism, which they saw as greedy, exploitive, and unduly competitive. It thrived on inequity, they said, and paid just enough to ensure a new generation of workers. Peddling the 1917 Soviet experiment, they said that Marx had been right—that workers needed to seize control of factories from wealthy owners, elect workers' councils (Soviets), and set their own pay scales and production plans.

This fifth column worked on behalf of and was sometimes remunerated by the US Communist Party and its international parent, the Comintern. Many leftist agents were organized and recruited, famously Whitaker Chambers and Alger Hiss, whose work on behalf of the Bolsheviks is recounted in *The Venona Secrets*. Their goal was to undermine the United States, to destabilize the existing order and pave the way to socialism. They managed to penetrate the US government at high levels and passed important classified information to Soviet leaders. In addition, and most importantly, they infiltrated the US educational system. Leftist academics gradually persuaded their students of capitalism's unfairness; these students included future teachers and journalists as well as many of our community neighbors.

Leftist academics intended to deconstruct America as understood by most of its citizens. Our myths were revised, emphasizing the immorality and corruption of our founding, and revision was also assisted by Hollywood leftists:

'Attempts at historical revision are apparent in many of our public schools and universities. It isn't far-fetched to imagine that this also takes place in entertainment offerings. ... We are losing history. ... The question arises: is this being done with dramatic license, from ignorance, or hostility toward our very foundations?' (7)

A few began to see the extent of the subversion. Senator Joseph McCarthy so informed the Congress (House Un-American Activities Committee) but was finally discredited by the press for his alcoholism, and his seemingly indiscriminate accusations of seditious behavior ("Senator, have you no sense of decency?" Joseph Nye Welch famously rebuked McCarthy for his tactics). Subversion continued. Journalists and entertainers, often leftists, expedited this subversion. Journalism's one-time motto, "Comfort the afflicted and afflict the comfortable," may explain their frequent opposition to capitalist wealth. Leftist editorialists and media journalists provided their own versions of United States history, current affairs, and the meaning of the news. For many, they are the sole source of information and analysis, and the general ignorance of the American audience makes it vulnerable to Leftist propaganda. Hollywood makes its own contribution to undermining the capitalist order with films critical of our history and highlighting capitalism's greed.

From leftist academics, subversion is spread to students and becomes standard pedagogic content for subsequent generations of teachers at all levels. Academia soon becomes the most influential leftist group. Their affinity for socialist thought is explained by Joseph Schumpeter (1950):

'The expansion of education in Capitalist societies produces an oversupply of the white-collar educated; many of these (arts and soft-science majors) have no salable skills and become the unemployed-educated, who then drift into the vocations in which the standards are least definite. ... They swell the host of intellectuals and enter it in a thoroughly discontented frame of mind, ... which accounts for their hostility to the Capitalist order.'(8)

As academia contributes large numbers of anti-capitalist Leftists, many teachers are increasingly convinced of socialism's attractions, and are able to persuade students of the benefits of ever-larger government. More taxation permits an enlarging welfare-state, promoting dependence on politicians, who buy votes with generous benefits paid for by hard-working citizens. As the politician's power grows, so does his wish to be reelected, and his need to buy more votes. Elected to make decisions which might compromise his reelection, he encourages the growth of an immense and expensive administrative bureaucracy which is unaccountable, and makes all the tough decisions for him. Gradually there is little connection between the voter and an accountable 'expert' who increasingly controls his life. A kind of soft despotism develops, about which de Tocqueville warned. The extent of government's intervention in our lives has been restrained by constitutional limitations, but the need to please the electorate by widening government's role in our lives eventually corrupts the judiciary and widens those limits. And so the constitutional restraints which were intended to protect us from an ever-larger and more intrusive federal government are slowly weakened by a judiciary anxious to be well-liked and part of the leftist chic.

'It was soon discovered that the forms of a free and the ends of a [despotic] government were things not altogether incompatible. That same discovery stands behind the growth of the American administrative state. Under the cloak of Democratic institutions, government pursues an expansionist agenda which threatens liberty … by circumventing the law'(9)

Americans have become wealthier than the rest of the world because of capitalism and a (relatively) small government. The average European has fewer (or no) cars and lives in a much smaller space. But America may not always be so rich, since politics in the United States has become a career, and the best path to reelection, our congress has discovered, is offering handouts to voters, who now expect 'free' benefits. Vote-buying and career politicians are good news to the political left, who see that an ever-enlarging and more generous government must end in bankruptcy, easing the move to socialism. 'Sharing the wealth', redistribution, and an unrealistic egalitarianism are socialist premises., to be funded (a) by insisting that wealthier citizens 'pay their fair share', (b) by borrowing from China, and (c) finally by overprinting paper money. So far, the 'rich' seem willing to pay, but they can be expected to finally sequester their wealth or leave the country.

'Here's the thing Liberals don't understand: the federal government is bloated; its been costing Americans too much for decades. We should be reducing government rather than increasing it. At some point the tax burden just becomes too much, especially for working families. They're best served by being able to keep more of their money' (10)

But politicians ignore this advice, and campaigns have become auctions: the highest bidder gets the votes. On the way to bigger government, expensive promises are made that can be delivered only at the risk of bankrupting America. Politicians who understand this are reluctant to tell us, for fear of losing elections, which are now more important to them than the country's wellbeing.

'[American political culture is an] … endless saturnalia of bunk, of bluff, of stupidity, of insincerity, of false virtue, of nonsense, of pretense, of sophistry … of bamboozlement, of auctorial posturing, of empty words, even, at times, of downright fraud'.—H. L. Mencken

'If you want your children to be politicians, teach them to lie, loudly and with conviction.'

—R. M. Winston-Salem Journal,

The liberal Left cannot reasonably be blamed for every minor unpleasantness in American life, but they often create or exploit social divisions. While they once operated as a fifth column, complete with foreign-supported conspirators and a subversive agenda, they are no longer to be thought of as a secret society conspiring against capitalism. Instead, overly ambitious politicians and leftist academics at all levels gradually persuade poorly educated voters that socialism offers a more comfortable life, despite historical evidence to the contrary. Capitalism has provided material wealth beyond most dreams, but our citizens, many thinly educated, are unaware of its importance to their well-being. Many are slowly persuaded that capitalism is unfair and greedy, and socialism is fair and compassionate. The capitalist order, the source of America's wealth, is undermined subtly by leftist media and academics. Liberals are perpetually aggrieved, never quite satisfied with the distribution of America's wealth; they insist that 'oppressed groups' remain, and something must be done.

Their commitment to subversion doesn't mean that all of America's leftists had to meet conspiratorially around a large table in Cambridge or New Haven; they needn't have communicated secretly by telephone or social media. Convincing our elites that the United States needs a revolution must have developed quite gradually during university lectures, tutorials, and postgraduate symposia. It was no doubt easier to subvert during economic downturns or unpopular wars, when student protests tended to agree with leftist faculty. Haydn wrote 'students and faculty must wrest control of the educational process from the administrative bureaucracy '(59) in 1962's Huron Manifesto, and students have been wresting ever since.

I B

The Leftist Merger With the DEMOCRATIC PARTY

(VOTE-BUYING, VEHEMENCE, and VIOLENCE)

JFK's inaugural advice was "don't ask what your country can do for you."(11) His Democratic Party, on merging with the Left, inverts his counsel and urges its voters to ask for ever greater wealth redistribution. Each election brings new "free" goodies from the government, which now distributes food, medical care, childcare, housing, educational loans, and more. John Kennedy's Democrats have gradually united with the American left and brought with them Marx's dream of a large socialist state. Our recent presidential candidates included an admitted socialist, a descriptor that in past campaigns would have disqualified him/her, but Senator Sanders openly advocated a generous statism to displace capitalism, which he rejects as avaricious. He hopes for a new social order—an egalitarian utopia that takes money from the rich and distributes it to low-earning voters; he sees expropriation as acceptable as long as it's called taxation. In return for this generosity to underachievers, leftist politicians expect votes. Quid-pro-quo tactics are a way to lasting political power, vote buying at its most effective. Reliable Democratic voting blocs must be organized, serviced, supported, and pampered; marginalized groups can be promised 'normalization', and those ostracized or oppressed are offered elevated self-esteem in return for their votes. America's disadvantaged, when properly organized, can change the traditional order on behalf of the left. The following groups have been chosen by the liberal left as reliable voters:

(a)Women who feel exploited or can be so persuaded
(b)People of color who feel exploited or can be so persuaded
(c)immigrants, legal and illegal
(d) LGBTQ

(e) the poor

These groups are designated by the Left as disadvantaged, historically damaged, socially marginalized, and victimized. While once America ranked its citizens according to achievement--say, in athletics or academics-it now grades them according to their degree of 'victimization', which has become an honorific, often prominently displayed.

'...many begin to think of themselves as victims. Indeed, they aspire to victim status...they seek the moral capital of victimhood...they tend to see their lives collectively as historical melodrama involving the forces of good and evil, in which they are cast as secular saints and martyrs...(minority groups) compete to establish themselves as the most oppressed of all. Everybody races to sieze the lowest rung of the ladder...minorities acquire a powerful moral claim that renders their opponents defensive and apologetic, and immunizes themselves from criticism and sanction. Ultimately, victimhood becomes a truncheon...(to)...intimidate nonminorities. Thus the victim becomes a victimizer...' (12) As it has seemed to merge with the Democrats, liberalism has presented itself as the savior of America's marginalized groups. Any demographic group feeling itself disadvantaged, or that can be persuaded so, has been united with others to strengthen the voting base and form a liberal Democratic army. And there are some voters who, emulating their grandfathers, continue to support the party, apparently not seeing its distinct move to the left. But by far the largest electoral support for Democrats comes from our liberal neighbors, those in our community, many of whom were taught by the anti-capitalist academics Schumpeter describes.

The leftist Democrats pledge to improve the lives of these disadvantaged groups, both by legislation and by public normalization; compliant news and entertainment industries will convince the larger US public that ostracism is unjustified and cruel and that a more enlightened attitude is required. Laws will be interpreted, or policies introduced, to protect each of these groups under the guise of sympathy for the underprivileged. The welfare state and government intervention will inevitably require further bureaucracy, augmenting an already sizeable Democratic voting bloc. The laws and programs protecting and elevating these groups will be presented to the public as entirely compassionate and altruistic; those who oppose them will be accused of bigotry, sexism, and white supremacy. But, especially with regard to immigrants, American pity may be misunderstood :

'...any clear-thinking observer can see that compassion is not a sound basis for either foreign policy or immigration policy. Compassion is more likely to lead to contempt than gratitude in both areas'(1)

Gradually, the Democratic Party has become the home of American Leftism. This is increasingly clear, and, while Leftism and the Socialist Goal were at first concealed, by increments and with increasing boldness, their commitment to a collectivist order has been confirmed, and some party leaders are now openly radical.

Increasingly, Democratic rhetoric is critical of America. Despte major steps forward in race relations, New jersey's Sen. Cory Booker declared that 'we are at a time when injustice has grown to be normal in our country... '.Senator Warren, ignoring the violence that is endemic to black ghettos, and their very high murder rate, offered '...the hard truth about our criminal justice system, its racist...I mean, all the way, front to back...Sen Kamala Harris joined the assault, telling netroots that 'our criminal justice has failed...Alexandria O Cortez, the Democratic-Socialist... told netroots that Immigration and Customs Enforcement (ICE)...has repeatedly, systematically, and violently committed human-rights abuses...she support(ed) free college, guaranteed jobs, and single-payer healthcare...'(13) Needless to say, continued rhetoric of this sort encourages and has been responsible for rioting, looting, arson, and many police deaths. Brett Kavanaugh's detractors insist that he will be impeached if confirmed as the ninth Supreme Court Justice. In California and elsewhere, resistance to federal authority is flaunted in sanctuary cities. Is this the beginning of Tytler's prediction of anarchy?

The ultimate goal of this political coalition (LGBTQ, minorities, immigrants, feminists, the poor, etc), remember, is to gradually subvert American capitalism. Once social problems are identified, generous programs will be established to resolve them; if successful, they will be touted by the Left as proof that ever-larger government works. If unsuccessful, the political right will be blamed for insufficient funding and time (and in any case, the Left may prefer the political issue to its solution). Finally, if the expense of the new program brings the United States closer to bankruptcy, so much the better.One estimate is that the US federal government has unfunded liabilities exceeding $150 trillion and counting(113). Borrowing is a short-term solution to funding, but interest payments alone finally begin to encroach on our GNP. Politicians must know that insolvency threatens, but they are loath to admit their improvidence. Spending must continue to buy votes and ensure reelection, and incumbents are gambling that bankruptcy won't be announced until after they retire

Programs, once established and funded by the federal government, never seem to die. One example is the Corporation for Public Broadcasting, a system with many affluent listeners and viewers, which could easily be supported by private advertising. But, persuaded that public funding was required, the Federal Gov't established NPR and PBS, and continues to subsidize this system with US taxes. The reliance on annual federal refunding politicizes the broadcasting, which finally serves as a Leftist voice to its audience. Racial division and identity politics are also taught by the Corporation for Public Broadcasting, since it:

'maintains a diversity development fund which has supported feminist (causes) and advises that "one's never too young to get woke" about race. Such programming continues to divide despite evidence that...program grants around specific identity groups isn't good for America' (14)

'As changing technologies and preferences make government-funded broadcasting increasingly preposterous, such broadcasting actually becomes useful by illustrating two dismal facts. One is the immortality of entitlements that especially benefit those among society's articulate upper-reaches, who feel entitled. The other fact is how impervious government programs are to evidence incompatible with their premises'. (15)

Those of us who believe that the central government should confine itself to financing foreign wars and interstate highways are finally overrun by voters who can't wait for Washington's newest handout. Democracy begins to fail, says Tytler, when citizens realize they can vote themselves benefits; national bankruptcy, which is an alternative leftist goal, often follows. Meantime, Democratic rhetoric claims that the rich aren't paying their fair share, and class division widens.

Continetti (16) says '... the Left's war against capitalism weakened when Soviet Socialism's coercion and brutality were publicized. A new battle plan was needed. Just as the Socialist movement had propagandized all of capitalism's alleged inadequacies (greed, exploitation, excessive competition), the new plan would concentrate on America's (and Europe's) historical transgressions, past and present: slavery and ongoing racism; unequal treatment of women; whitesupremacy and contempt for non-whites generally, especially immigrants; maltreatment of LGBT people; and any other "disadvantaged" or "oppressed" group.'

A measure of how far left the Democrats has deviated since, say, JFK's administration is shown by some of the Democratic Party's recent decisions: (a) They booed the inclusion of God in their 2012 platform, (b) they would permit bathroom use according to stated gender preference, (c) they would force small businesses and nuns to cover abortion drugs, despite their beliefs, (d) they forced the resignation of an executive who opposed gay marriage, and (e) they fined a small bakery more than $140,000 for refusing a wedding cake to a homosexual couple (32)

The left uses identity politics to divide and conquer. Hear Mark Lilla: 'White men have one (way of seeing the world), and black women another....this view threatens to undermine the idea that any politician can successfully represent any voter except those of the same color and culture. It suggests that representative democracy is fundamentally unworkable.Can a politician represent constituents of drastically different background...? '(99)

II

Utopian Dreams

'I'll build a stairway to paradise
With a new step every day
I'm going to get there at any price
Stand aside, I'm on my way' George Gershwin, 'An American in Paris'

Many years ago, there was a radio program called *Let's Pretend*, in which children enacted wish-fulfillment fairy tales. Had the program survived, the script would surely now be written by the political Left, who pretend that (a) all people are equal, (b) they are fundamentally virtuous, and (c) any minor corruption is due to capitalism and "social constructs," ; we can, shades of Rousseau, eliminate their defects and proceed to the perfect social order.

Somebody said that most people live their lives in a kind of quiet desperation. Maybe that explains mankind's recurrent efforts to define and locate the perfect place and way to live. In Classical mythology it was the Golden Age … a period of serenity, peace, and eternal spring (ColumbiaEncyclopedia)1947. In the Christian era, we're calling it Eden or paradise, and we look forward to our arrival there. In the meantime, there is an ongoing search for a terrestrial utopia.

In the early sixteenth century, Thomas More named the perfect place "Utopia," "where all is ordered for the best of mankind as a whole, and misery and poverty have been done away with" (Columbia Encyclopedia 1947). By the mid-nineteenth century, Karl Marx offered his own utopian vision: a workers' paradise to come, where bosses and hierarchy would be abolished, and workers will produce for themselves, at their own pace. This particular dream has become the Left's favorite fantasy; striving for Marx' Socialist paradise has had enormous influence worldwide and has often led to revolution. During the Great Depression (1929–41), Marxist ideas seemed especially attractive. The gap between rich and poor was proof to many that capitalism rewarded only the avaricious, usually at the expense of the exploited poor. The 1917 Soviet experiment became chic among America's intellectuals, and Alger Hiss (among others) began working for Socialism on behalf of the Bolshevik government. Academics who were "hostile to the Capitalist order" embraced Socialism and began persuading young American students to prefer its promise of "social justice", which would include wealth-sharing and a perfected egalitarianism.

'(The Leninist) vanguard believed they knew what was best for the working class and should use its irrefutable knowledge of the world … to hasten the advent of the perfect society on earth" (6)

Utopian persuasion remains with us: "Socialism promises all these amazing things, like free education, free healthcare, and a living wage" (28).

Liberal utopianism is very seductive, especially for those who ignore its failures and don't understand that socialism's implementation in the United States would make most of us much poorer, denying us capitalism's material advantages. When Bernie Sanders promises benefits, his listeners need to understand that (a) political pledges go mostly unfulfilled, and (b) utopia is finally just a dream. While some may think that combining the best part of capitalism (material wealth) with the best of socialism (redistribution of wealth) can be effected, the truth is that the two systems are mutually exclusive. Socialism can't provide the material plenty found in Capitalism, in part because governmental control of production tends to be incompetent. Eastern Europe has been under socialist influence to its detriment:

'(while)… the newly industrialized countries of the third world are building factories with the most advanced technology, Socialist Eastern Europe is increasingly a museum of the early industrial age. … Eastern Europe is rapidly becoming part of the third world, … and many third world countries are surpassing it economically. … Singapore, an Asian city with only 2 million residents, exports 20 percent more machinery to the West than all of Socialist Eastern Europe.' (29)

Socialism and Communism were abysmal failures in the twentieth century, especially since the "Grand Failure" of the 1917 Russian experiment. Collectivism fails, Bork explains(20), because (a) collectivization is opposed by many (not all want the same thing), and (b) coercion is finally required, which is responsible for an estimated 100 million twentieth-century deaths. (Courtois 1997) Despite these failures, and because many Americans are thinly educated, socialist promises remain seductive; limited education promotes vulnerability to Utopian leftist humbug:

…"I don't think my fellow young people really understand what Socialism is. To most of us, it's an abstract concept, identified more with the "lovable crazy uncle" image of Bernie Sanders than the tyranny of Stalin" (28) Many of America's young wish for "…a world where we don't have to sell our labor because so much will be provided for us…." Again,…, "while they might detest Capitalism, they have no intention of giving up the technology that represents its most brutally efficient form" (ibid). False promises attract many to leftism; others, says Schueck (30), are attracted by envy: Those who fail under capitalism can't bear to see it provide success to others and would rather replace it.

 Pollution, poverty, and crime, says the left, are all products of social injustice" and emphasize capitalism's exploitation of the poor and 'victimized'. The "global warming" movement is, as Rosen(28) points out, primarily anti-capitalist. Our numerous factories, they say, are fed by fossil fuels and are contaminating the air we breathe. Destroying private enterprise would save us all. A collectivist state that did away with inequality would solve our problems; crime, poverty, and prisons would disappear, and police might no longer be necessary. If egalitarianism ruled, a more loving and sympathetic economic system would define the new Socialist order. But the coercion required to effect collectivization is anything but compassionate. Stalin, for example, mandated that wealthy peasant-farmers donate their crop to the state; those who declined often found themselves at the bottom of their own wells.

Anticapitalists remain in control in many countries. ... The philosophy 'remains' a force around the world. Many anticapitalists embrace violence as a legitimate tool and believe that the end justifies the means. The US has experienced this violence first-hand with ... 'anticapitalists protesting and shutting down speech.' This embrace of violence by Anticapitalists is perhaps strongest at our universities. In 100 Years of Communism--and 100 Million Dead," David Satter concludes that "the independent authority of universal moral principle is the conviction on which all civilization depends. ... [He] laments that Individual conscience was subordinated to "Soviet Power."(31)

In spite of this brutal history, Leftism remains enticing, and the utopian dream dies hard. Especially in America, where we are tempted daily by expensive goods and beautiful people we cannot afford; it is no surprise that we finally succumb to dreaming of a generous social order where all will be equal, hierarchy dead, and competition erased. Each will receive an equal share of whatever is produced, and 'social justice' will reign. The trouble is that people are not equal, and all of us are subject to the tyranny of the bell-curve. Those on the far left of the curve will always underperform those well to the right, no matter how much we pretend otherwise.

'Equality of opportunity comes to grief because all individuals do not have the same ability to make use of their opportunities with equal or comparable success" (30).

III

Leftism's Adverse Effects: an Overview of Leftist Social Policy

'Thinking Americans have turned away from Democrats because we know their ultimate goal is power and control. They want to make everything political; they've made sex, ... climate, ... education, success, free speech, ... poverty,... and employment political. ... Some of us, but not all, take responsibility for ourselves ... When you pass laws (benefitting) the least responsible and stupidest among us, then you alienate those of us who do take responsibility'.(33)

'The root cause of the left's disease is that it has abandoned truth for power. The central teachings of the Left (welfare cures poverty, only whites can be racist, capitalism is oppressive, gender is malleable, abortion is just a choice, unions help workers, trace levels of CO_2 control the climate) are false, no matter how often they are repeated. Progressive policies (socialized medicine, taxing the rich, alternative energy, centralized control of the economy) don't work, no matter how often they're tried...Liberals never admit what they're doing is wrong, they just insist that they haven't done enough of it yet...'(34)

The liberal Left hopes to undermine the American belief in its capitalist order. Effecting Obama's "fundamental transformation," they are at pains to disrupt parts of American sociopolitical culture, some of which seemed to have been working fairly well. Insisting on "social justice," leftist policies have often had effects contrary to those ostensibly intended; they have reopened wounds that seemed on the mend. Hostile feelings about slavery, Jim Crow, and ongoing discrimination against blacks seemed, after 150 years, to be diminishing, and it looked as if black and white might finally be able to work together amicably. Instead, the Left has stoked that enmity and purposely reawakened black-white animosity for its own political advantage.

Leftism urged "normalization" of LGBT groups, previously marginalized and ostracized. In so doing, they've exposed the greater population to a higher incidence of many diseases, some of which are quite deadly. By lionizing feminism, they've put chips on lots of female shoulders and denigrated masculinity. Men and women are increasingly confused about traditional social and parental roles, and many find it difficult to form a conventional male-female partnership. The Left is in love with what it thinks of as science, but, as I hope to show, often misunderstands its meaning. Their few successful programs are applauded as proof that big government is to be preferred when a social problem needs solving. Many of their programs, however, have been expensive failures. (For their purposes, failure is as good as success, especially as bankruptcy threatens.)

In its frenzy to fundamentally transform, the Left is undoing America. The road to utopia, to paraphrase Judge Bork (1996), is littered with the remnants of conservative capitalism's most useful policies. Transformation requires coercion, which can become "nasty and violent." Further, the Left seems committed to "scientific solutions," usually meaning sociologic nostrums that conform to leftist prejudgment; wishful thinking has become pseudoscience, and social actions based on it often have adverse effects. Consider the Left's insistence that black disparity in economic achievement must be due to discrimination by the white majority:

'Any serious study of racial and ethnic groups, whether in a given society or in a wide variety of societies in countries around the world, repeatedly encounters the inescapable fact of large and numerous disparities among these groups, whether in income, education, crime rates, IQ, or many other things. These differences cannot be dismissed as … maltreatment by others, as was often cited in the late twentieth century.' (35)

Ignoring this information, leftist dogma insists that disparities in the United States are due to racism, which perpetuates black poverty and, therefore, crime. So, despite knowing that 50 percent of US murders are caused by 6 percent of its population (black men), liberals want us to believe that the ultimate cause of high crime in black communities is white bigotry. Political correctness prevents acknowledging that Afro-American poverty and crime are products of an anti-intellectual, fatherless, and often criminal black subculture.

Is the Left correct? Does poverty cause crime? If so, how to explain that San Francisco's Chinatown, for example, was at once its poorest and most crime-free neighborhood? As for discrimination, why is it that, despite strong anti-Chinese feeling among whites, many Chinese immigrants' children proceeded to excel at our best Universities? (51). In New Zealand, says Dalrymple (46), crime increased as poverty diminished.

'Poverty and discrimination thus don't account for the rise in New Zealand's crime rate, (which) provides no support for liberal theories of crime…It is true, of course, that the decision of criminals to commit their crimes must have antecedents; but they are not to be found in New Zealand's poverty, unemployment, or inequality...'

It remains to the benefit of the Left, however, to claim that 'white supremacy' explains black failure and that a generous welfare program is required to reduce poverty, and therefore crime. Nathan Glazer, a Harvard sociologist, assisted LBJ in designing the Great Society (much as Harvard and other faculties had 'masterminded' the Vietnam war), and for over fifty years, more than $22 trillion was transferred from Washington to poor communities in the United States as part of the War on Poverty. Some will say that LBJ had vote-buying in mind, but Glazer's altruism seems to have been genuine. The results of this great experiment in prolonged welfare are discouraging, as even Glazer and Moynihan finally saw. Instead of becoming productive, tax-paying citizens, the beneficiary communities are now better known for drug trafficking, addiction, riots, and violent crime, especially murder. South Chicago was the site of sixty-five shootings and thirteen deaths over Labor Day weekend 2016. There is much evidence by now that welfare programs encouraging single-motherhood increase crime among young black males. But there has been no serious effort to gradually diminish or discontinue these programs and their attendant bureaucracies. On the contrary, any effort to reduce these neighborhood subsidies is attacked by a strong welfare lobby and a race industry that thrives on handouts and the political patronage they create. By now, handouts have created a dependent underclass that for several generations has had its work ethic eroded. Any interruption in this largesse threatens civil unrest.

Those initially responsible for the War on Poverty are long dead, and current leftist politicians won't admit this costly error. They've insulated themselves by hiring "experts" who can be blamed. A major liberal social experiment has failed, and the failure goes unacknowledged. For the Democrats, this hasn't been a total loss; the War on Poverty continues to subsidize recipients of welfare, a now-dependent subculture forming a liberal-Democratic base. The Democratic Left will enlarge that political base by adding unvetted, illegal Central American, Mexican, and middle-Eastern immigrants, once again expanding its dependent voting bloc.

The dependent poor-white and African-American population created by prolonged welfare subsidies is vulnerable to anti-capitalist and anti-white propaganda from the racism industry. Jackson, Sharpton, & Co. have declared blacks victims of white supremacy and encouraged rioting that has destroyed black communities. After Trayvon Martin's shooting by police in Sanford, Florida, and again following Michael Brown in Ferguson, Missouri, President Obama could have urged civil calm and obedience. Instead, he personalized one incident ('He could have been my son'), and did very little to prevent the rioting and burning which ensued. Riots are a major source of community demise and the ghetto poverty which results:

'...(a) the poverty rate among Detroit's black population before the riots was only half that of blacks nationwide, (b) the home ownership rates among blacks in Detroit was the highest in the nation, and (c) the unemployment rate of blacks in Detroit was 3.4 percent, lower than that among whites nationwide…It was after the riots that Detroit became a ravaged community, and remained so for decades thereafter, as businesses withdrew, taking jobs and taxes with them.'(35)

We shouldn't be surprised by the failure of LBJ's Great Society. Politicians and even sociologists, as Goldberg points out, often confuse wishing with empiricism. Even Nathan Glazer, originally optimistic that LBJ's Great Society might reduce poverty and therefore crime among American minorities, finally admitted that the policy had serious adverse effects. "I came to believe that social policy … had given rise to other problems no less grave " ("Limits of Social Policy"). He and Daniel Patrick Moynihan recognized the erosion of work ethic and family integrity among recipients. Other government interventions have been equally adverse. Consider that unemployment rates for black teenagers were lower than whites until the passage of minimum-wage legislation:

'The last year in which black unemployment was lower than white,… 1930 … was also the last year in which there was no federal minimum-wage law' (35)

The new law resulted in job losses for many blacks, and it might be said that it marked the beginning of Detroit's decline to the empty lots and broken windows seen today. Government interference with free-market forces is a leftist device, and even when intended as egalitarian and compassionate, "social engineering" often produces contrary effects:

"Minimum wage laws are … as clear a case as one can find of a measure the effects of which are precisely the opposite of those intended by men of good will who support it" (52)

Charity of any kind, but especially when given without conditions (e.g., workfare) and over long periods, has a deleterious effect on work ethic. V. Olasky (53)believes it is a cause of pauperism, especially when administered by central governments, which (a) cannot evaluate the true need for assistance at the local level, (b) employ large bureaucracies that become self-perpetuating and self-augmenting, and (c) politicize it and tend to buy voters with handouts.It is prone to corruption from above and cheating from below. Charity should be dispensed locally, probably by churches, and workfare should be required whenever possible. The Great Society and its War on Poverty have failed; instead of productive citizens, it has yielded drug dealers and crime-prone neighborhoods. Rather than admit failure, the Left has continued the War on Poverty, and its adverse influences persist in communities where America's frank unraveling may begin. Leftist dogma, in this case the belief that poverty and crime can be eliminated by government largesse, is never extinguished.

The *subsidiarity* principle argues that social problems should be dealt with at the smallest and most local level possible. Administering welfare, for example, might be performed by (a) church, (b) neighborhood leaders, (c) family, (d) in some cases, ethnic identity groups or (e) government, local, state, or federal. Subsidiarity recognizes that local administration has the advantage of evaluating recipients and their needs up close and, with a limited local budget, tends to eliminate shirking and confirm work requirements. State and federal governments and their agents, by contrast, can't easily evaluate needs or work performed. Large budgets encourage agents to recruit more of the "needy," thus inflating their use of assistants and their wages. The political Left rejects subsidiarity, requests overgenerous funding and, finally, ever-larger bureaucracy, a source of political patronage and votes. A basic difference between Left and Right is just that: the Left wants ever-larger government, and the Right would prefer smaller. Big government seems to be winning:

'Increasingly, most have voted for expanded government. As a result, the nation's leaders obediently begin debating laws about issues that should be reserved for personal or local judgment. … The list of such issues is almost infinite. A Library of Congress website listing government branch websites says it succinctly: "With the time we have available, it is not possible to list every department agency.' (37)

'The federal government has expanded into many areas that should be left to state and local governments, businesses, charities, and individuals. That expansion is sucking the life out of the private economy and creating a top-down bureaucratic society that is alien to American traditions… cutting federal spending would enhance civil liberties by dispersing power from Washington.'(from Downsizing the Federal Government website).

Beware of governments offering help: solving local problems becomes very expensive when they're involved. It's a bit like the guy who offers to repair your grandmother's roof and then sends a bill she can't afford to pay. There is an almost inevitable growth of large government, especially when your representatives approach with the phrase "Let us take care of that problem for you." Most of us are too busy with our own lives to notice the encroachment of federal or state government on local affairs. It is easy for the voter to acquiesce to these ultimately very expensive offers, especially when they believe, naively, that their political representatives are avuncular, altruistic, and working for the common weal. But this is the very thing de Tocqueville warned against:

'Citizens (might) surrender their freedom without a struggle when a subtle version of despotism surfaces to foresee and supply necessities, manage personal concerns, direct industry, and divide inheritances: Why should …(the citizenry)…not entirely relieve itself from the trouble of thinking and all the cares of living?' (55)

Governments have money only through taxing, borrowing, or printing. But to those who pay no income tax and aren't much aware of taxes withheld, the source of government funds takes on almost a mystical quality, and its limits are poorly defined. Even the well-educated may think transcendentally about the nation's wealth. The naive and ill-informed are especially vulnerable when large government offers to solve local problems. They often perceive their political representatives as devoid of self-interest and seem unaware of the cost of more bureaucracy. And, if Schueck and Levite are correct, the envious among us enjoy seeing the wealthy pay higher taxes, and so may welcome more bureaucracy. The liberal Left, meanwhile, is happy to see bigger government.

'US Representatives spend money on unnecessary programs all the time, and taxpayers absorb the cost because each item individually seems small. ... Much of the cost will be passed on to future generations.' (56)

Government absorbs wealth like an enormous sponge; its need for more money is unending. New funds might come from (a) higher taxes on the wealthy, (b) more borrowing, or (c) printing of unbacked paper currency. The affluent are already overtaxed; if pressed further, they will find ways to shelter their funds or flee the country. Capital Flight from the United States has already lost us two large businesses, Burger King and Pfizer. Low interest rates and overprinting paper money threaten increased inflation.

Polybius and others believed in historical cycles and evolving forms of government. As they saw it, monarchy fades to aristocracy, which finally becomes democracy; when voters begin voting themselves benefits, democracy gives way to anarchy. Attempting to restore order, despotism finally prevails, followed by a second monarchy. Some recent developments in the United States verge on the anarchic. Cities in California and New York, among many others, declare themselves "sanctuaries" for illegal immigrants in violation of federal law. In San Francisco, public urination and defecation are tolerated, suggesting anarchy has already arrived. At Berkely, students confusing freedom of speech with freedom of arson have burned university buildings, apparently without punishment. The president's orders denying entry to potential Islamic terrorists are not obeyed. Rioting and rampage in Baltimore are justified by its mayor as therapeutic, temporarily relieving black citizens of repressed anger due to historical oppression.(even politicians benefit from Freud's pseudoscientific 'insights').

Our founders were quite aware of government's tendency to enlarge itself and finally starve an economy; most money paid in taxes is removed from Adam Smith's capitalist market, while the wealth of those administering government increases. Affluence diminishes as government grows (per-capita automobile ownership in quasi-socialist Britain is, for example, markedly less than in the United States). Big government is very costly and not easy to reduce. Once installed, bureaucrats will fight fiercely to retain their positions, not always remaining within the law. Ben Franklin et al. left us a Republic and challenged us to keep it if we can, but bureaucracies and lobbyists will fiercely defend their turfs and have it within their power to make our lives very uncomfortable. So far, most of us have not felt the brutality of central government whose existence is challenged. But in Wisconsin, Governor Scott Walker's conservative supporters were subjected to midnight searches and seizures and initially denied legal counsel. Also, many conservative Tea Party groups were denied tax-deductibility by a leftist IRS. If the Wisconsin and IRS Democrats had been wearing brown shirts, the analogy with Fascist Germany would have been even more convincing.

Politicians have discovered that, by appointing "experts" before making expensive social-policy decisions, they can exonerate themselves if the new policy goes badly. So, despite their commission to personally decide social policy, they often insulate themselves from criticism by deferring to social "experts." In addition to adding considerable expense, this method removes accountability. Hence the growth of the administrative state, where seemingly autonomous agencies establish work rules that (a) should not have been made without the advice of business owners, (b) have a consistent anti-business bias, and (c) make life increasingly difficult for capitalists. Criticism aimed at the politician will simply be referred to the expert, who is unelected, therefore unaccountable, and perhaps immune to censure. Our political representatives, attempting to insulate themselves from failure, have interposed an administrative state between us and them, and it begins to feel like a marital separation: We find ourselves wondering if our welfare remains their primary concern and if they haven't abandoned their commitment to the country's wellbeing.

'The political class can bemoan [the election of President Trump]—the veteran journalists, the senators and governors, the administrators of the federal government, but this is a good time to remind ourselves that it was the failures of the political class that brought our circumstances about'. (57)

'What's vitiating our politics, in [F. H. Buckley's] view, is corruption. Americans hate their politicians not so much because they disagree with them but because they sense, often correctly, that the politicians are in it for themselves'. (58)

Big government is surely leftism's most dangerous adverse effect. Leftism mandates ever-larger government, which increases incessantly. Any problem that presents itself to liberals and their politicians is thought to be best dealt with by enlarging government's size and expense. Seemingly no thought is given to the added expense to taxpayers of new programs and bureaucracies. And, once created, the programs never die. Indeed, like cancer, they grow. Entitlement programs in particular expand, often, it appears, to enlarge support for the sponsoring politician.

'The pattern of expansion is remarkably common. New programs initially target benefits to a group of individuals deemed particularly worthy at the time. Eventually the excluded come forth to assert that they are no less worthy of aid and pressure lawmakers to relax eligibility rules. This ever-present pressure has been magnified...by the imperative of lawmakers and presidents to be elected and reelected...the Medicaid and foodstamp programs followed a similar path...originally limited to supplement welfare cash assistance...(they)...now extend aid to large segments of the population who are not on cash welfare and in some cases above the poverty line…Medicaid assists 25% of the non-elderly population. Foodstamps pay a major part of the grocery bills for 14% of the nonelderly population'(36)

As Tytler (38) reminds us: Democracy works until people begin to vote themselves benefits, then dissolves as bankruptcy threatens.

'"Spend now, pay later" is a well-travelled congressional path that has brought the country massive federal budget deficits and a staggering national debt…'(36)

Printing money in large amounts without much backing is what killed the Weimar Republic, and was a major cause of WWII. The Left cannot fail to see imminent bankruptcy in the United States as paving the way to a final financial and economic chaos leading to anarchy, democratic capitalism to be replaced by socialism.Chaos, as they see it, will hasten what they believe is an inevitable evolution from democracy to the liberal-leftist collectivist, statist utopian ideal, completing another arc of the historical cycle.

IV

Pseudoscience and the LEFT

There is widespread indifference to truth-seeking in current social science.—Paul Goss

'It would be difficult to exaggerate the deterioration suffered by the socialsciences, especially sociology … over the past forty years. … [Sociology] today is … larded with tendentious ideological beliefs assumed as facts'(78)

At least since the philosophic enlightenment (1715-89), humanity has committed itself to understanding causes and effects, empirical methods of experimentation, and believing that science must be the answer to man's need to improve himself and his environment. Science has indeed proved essential to bettering life. But "science" is not always scientific. Sometimes, in haste to explain a difficult problem or arrive at a desired solution, the meaning of "science" may be corrupted, and incorrect conclusions are reached, often those devoutly wished by the left. These conclusions, often politically motivated, become the basis of government policy, which (a) can be extremely expensive, and (b) may produce effects contrary to those seemingly intended. Clearly, it would be desirable to design social policy on a scientific foundation, and sociology is the proper science. Trouble is, sociology is itself in trouble, even among sociologists. Reproducibility of study results is essential to authenticating findings, but most sociologic studies are not replicable:

'The Center for Open Science was able to reproduce only thirty-nine of one hundred leading psychology experiments" …(and *Nature* found that)… "More than 70 percent of researchers have tried and failed to reproduce another scientist's experiments … more than half have failed to reproduce their own experiments" (79)

A leading cause of error is 'Confirmation bias', an investigator's prejudgment of the issue at question.

'The logic of validation in the social sciences is identical to that of the other sciences. But reproducibility involves many subjective variables, and is so vulnerable to confirmation bias, that sociology has rightly been termed "soft science." When politics enters sociology, the results are more likely to reflect "wishing and wanting" than objectivity and truth. ... Study results are often due to "confirmation bias," i.e., the examiner's predisposition when approaching the problem in question.' (80)

Transgendered people, for example, have been chosen by the liberal Left as one of its "disadvantaged" groups, and the Left has attempted to socially ameliorate this group in return for their votes. Amelioration requires normalization and convincing the larger public that transgenderism should no longer be thought of as grotesque or as a lifestyle choice but rather like a disease.Just as we would feel compassion toward cancer victims, says the Left, so must we accept transgenders, doing our best to "normalize" them. They are, after all, victims of a genetic disorder recently (and conveniently) discovered and verified by the left, with "scientific" proof. 'Breakthrough discoveries', especially in the social sciences, should raise our eyebrows and make us suspect mendacious science. Another example is alcoholism; once it was proclaimed a 'disease', not simply irresponsible behavior, it was only a matter of time before a 'genetic disposition' would be discovered and promoted by social scientists, exonerating the drunkard of any responsibility for his behavior. Once it had been 'proven in the laboratory' and encouraged by the left, government rehabilitation programs were inevitable. Generous government funding and a bureaucracy would be devoted to reducing US drunkenness, and those benefitting would be expected to support the sponsoring politicians, probably members of the democratic left.

Evaluating the scientific basis for sociologic studies is essential to predicting if proposed social programs will be beneficial. Understanding empiricism as pursuing knowledge by observation and experiment will assist in foresight. Is crime due to poverty? Is alcoholism a disease? Does psychoanalysis cure murderers? How should we decide if (a) causes (b)? Austin B. Hill, a British statistician (81), described seven criteria, which, if fulfilled, indicate a very strong likelihood that two events are causally related. They are as follows:

(1) The causative event (a) must precede the result (b)
(2) A very strong correlation between (a) and (b) must be found.
(3) the likelihood of (b) must increase with the amount of (a), and vice versa.
(4) the association between (a) and (b) must be consistent in all studies and among various populations
(5) the association must not violate our current understanding of sociologic/pathologic processes
(6) alternate explanations of cause and effect must be considered.
(7) the causation must be replicable or preventable in appropriate experiments.

(8) a single cause must explain a specific effect; this criterion is weak, since most effects are due to multiple causal factors

(9) coherence: must we reject current understanding of social processes in order to accept this causation?

Not all "science" meets these criteria, and conclusions are often contaminated by (a) confirmation bias, and (b) confusing correlation with causation: (a) Social scientists have often prejudged experimental findings, and this prejudgment may be "confirmed" by a slightly distorted perception of the results(b) Correlation doesn't always mean causation: the rooster crows as the sun rises, but the crowing hasn't caused the sunrise. Sociopolitical ideology may alter a social scientist's perception of an experimental result, and correlation may imply causation that doesn't exist. Both these sources of error should be eliminated when "studies" in soft science are evaluated.

'One need merely skim the publications ... to see that they engender the purest form of the victory of wish and ideology over the willingness to take truth as it comes'(80)

. Proving causation requires empiricism, meaning evaluation of a testable prediction(78). The prediction must be tested experimentally, and establishing causation between (a) and (b)must be consistent with Hill's criteria. The left's attempt to destigmatize transgenderism, as an example, seems overly convenient and may reflect pseudoscience:

'A massive cultural shift over the last couple of years has transformed transgenderism from curiosity to the conventional. And, right on cue, science discovers that to be trans is the biological norm. Wow! What are the odds? ... Could it be that scientists are eager to chase trends as a way to chase grants? Perhaps. And they may wish to avoid ... career-ending opprobrium, ... trying to publish ... conclusions inconsistent with the morals of the moment. ... The advocates of the new gender-identity movement can justify their agenda not just as a civil-rights cause but as an imperative demanded by scientific consensus. (82)

The Left adopts sociology and its findings with uncritical enthusiasm, especially when its findings coincide with their desired result. They create policies according to sociologic "studies," which, unfortunately, may not accurately predict human behavior. Will prolonged and overgenerous welfare subsidies eliminate poverty and crime? Apparently not, but some sociologic 'studies' in the mid-60s supported that idea. Just as when planning the "Great Society and the War on Poverty", leftists persist in quoting poorly performed studies to justify their social policies. They much admire Sigmund Freud, many of whose hypotheses are untestable, and whose conclusions don't fulfil Hill's criteria.

Since the release of Freud's letters by his daughter, there has been strong evidence (especially from his detractors) that (a) he was a cocaine addict, and (b) many of his "insights" came while he was heavily drugged. Many have concluded that much of his work is meaningless. Even before the letters were released, there were well-founded reasons for seeing his work as unscientific. Despite his recent discreditation, he has left us with an almost unshakeable series of 'psychoanalytic insights' which often cloud our minds with nonsense; some call it 'psychobabble'.

The problem lies in empiricism, which insists that predictions must be testable, andcause-and-effect must be demonstrable. Much of Freud's work depended upon highly subjective, non-verifiable, non-reproducible observations. This problem is even more complex given human duplicity. Trying to evaluate the results of talking therapy, the psychoanalyst might ask, "Are you feeling better since our last session?" An answer of "yes" may indicate (a) he's actually feeling better, or (b) he has a need to please the therapist,. A "no" answer, Freud thought, might not mean he wasn't feeling better, but that the patient was "resisting" therapy. In many cases, positive and negative responses were given equal meaning, a clear violation of Hill's criteria of causation. Take, for example, the question, "Are you homosexual?" An affirmative answer will be taken as evidence that the patient is in fact homosexual; but the same conclusion was reached when homosexuality was denied, since it was assumed that the patient was 'resisting'. Inferring the same conclusion from opposing bits of evidence violates Hill's criteria.

Despite the unprovable aspects of Freud's "insights," many on the Left find his pseudoscience useful and are especially fond of its inferences about parenting and antisocial behavior, which they present as hard science. Since his disciples saw criminals as products of abusive parenting, they are to be considered ill, and their crimes seen as the product of that illness; absolved of any evil intent, goes the thinking, they need rehabilitation, not punishment. Antisocial behavior, then, is the fault of the criminal's parents, and eliminates guilt in the criminal. But it also encourages further crime, as Dalrymple (2001) writes:

'It is impossible to state precisely when the Zeitgeist changed and the criminal became a victim in the minds of intellectuals; not only history, but the history of an idea, is a seamless robe… but in 1966, … Norman Mailer and J.P. Sartre portrayed criminals as existential heroes in revolt against a heartless, inauthentic world … the moral of the story is that those who go to court and to prison are victims of chance at best and prejudice at worst. … Such an attitude … prevents them from reflecting upon their own contribution to their predicament'. (Dalrymple 2001, 2009–10)

It also prevents meaningful punishment. The truth is, crime is a complex problem, and we don't understand it well. And since we seem unable to reliably change the criminal's habits and attitudes, then the causes of his crime matter only in an academic sense. For practical social purposes, he should be considered simply bad, evil, corrupt; harsh punishment and death penalties should be imposed when appropriate. The left's compassion should be directed to crime's victims, not the criminals. But the political left benefits from portraying murderers and thieves as victims of

Capitalism's greed and "white oppression" and this subversive dogma continues. Unpunished crime leads to more of the same, and the inability of the Capitalist order to protect its citizens undermines its authority. Softness on crime is a leftist attitude founded on sociologic 'studies':

'Sociologic Literature is inundated with the manipulation of flighty studies to prove some larger point about mankind in the name of behavioral science. Pop psychologists have churned out mountains of books proving some intuitive point that turns out to be wrong. It's "sciency" with a whiff of false authenticity…Its easy to write this off as trivial, except millions take these studies and their conclusions seriously' (79)

It is dogma on the Left that poverty causes crime. Therefore, they say, look what the government can do by way of a welfare state: we will eliminate not only poverty but crime as well. They are addicted to expensive programs that intend to create utopia with money. Governmental intervention and lots of taxpayer money can, they believe, accomplish anything. If a huge bureaucracy is needed, so be it; bureaucracies are one way to redistribute the taxes of the wealthy, and may become useful voting blocs. After fifty years of the War on Poverty, we may conclude that money doesn't erase poverty, much less prevent drime. As to eliminating the need for police, hear Dalrymple

'The idea that a juster social order would render the police redundant is utopian nonsense. A reliable and trustworthy police force is not a denial of freedom, but a precondition of its exercise. For those who doubt it, I can only recommend the last lines of Pablo Neruda's poem of the Spanish Civil War:
"Come and see the blood running thru the streets
;Come and see the blood running thru the streets"(50)

Poverty and crime tend to occur together (a correlation); but correlation is not causation. To conclude that poverty causes crime is probably incorrect. How can one explain that Chinatown was simultaneously the poorest and least criminal of San Francisco's neighborhoods (51) How do we explain that New Zealand crime rates increased with affluence, violating one of Hill's criteria(50) The correlation between crime and poverty might as easily mean that crime causes poverty, and that those who choose a criminal lifestyle are often broke: think pickpockets and petty thieves.

Ignoring that prolonged charity seems actually to increase crime rates, the left continues to insist that poverty causes crime, and alleviating poverty will reduce crime. Prolonged welfare in this form, it's now recognized (a) destroys the work ethic, and (b) removes the father from the home, so that young boys' violent impulses are not constrained.One major difference between the political left and right concerns the belief that people's basic nature is modifiable. The right believes that some people are fundamentally evil (lacking a better word) and remain so despite current attempts at psychotherapeutic "intervention." True to its conviction that people can be basically altered by adherence to Freud's "discoveries," the left thinks that criminals are victims of flawed parenting, and that prisons, instead of punishing, should become mental-health centers where rehabilitation is the primary goal. Despite statistical information that not much rehabilitation occurs, the left (and its sister organ, the ACLU) urges that prisoners be pampered, and that therapeutic talking will reduce recidivism. But some men are brutish, bestial, and it misleads the general public to suggest that they can be rehabilitated so as to justify parole.

Can talking therapies (cognitive behavioral therapy, CBT) prevent recidivism among violent criminals and predict which of them may be safely paroled? Apparently not very well: Despite rehabilitation, 54 percent of murderers commit crime after release, and 15 percent repeat violent crime (84) While some of us worry about that 15 percent, the left will advertise the remaining 85 percent as firm evidence that rehabilitation works. The left is at great pains to explain that criminals are not "evil" but victims of incompetent and abusive parenting; this thinking may be partly correct, but is of little practical importance; short of redoing defective childhoods, how does this reduce crime?. If more than 50 percent of murderers recidivate, what good is rehabilitation? It may be intellectually satisfying to believe that poor parenting induces crime, but this belief seems of little practical value, since poor parenting is not reversible. If the Freudian construct is correct that crime is a product of disease, how does that change our approach to reducing crime? Is the public safer after criminal rehabilitation, or are we just making ourselves feel better? Do we really believe perpetrators should be "rehabilitated" rather than punished, especially when recidivism rates remain high? Is that the best way to protect the public? If recidivism rates remain high even after rehabilitation, it seems clear that our "experts" are misnamed. Some men behave as beasts, and will remain so despite our commitment to 'scientific rehabilitation'. And while it may be comforting to believe that crime is well-understood, and 'scientifically' modifiable, the general public is endangered by premature parole. Crime without punishment is inconsistent with sensible governing, and leftist scientific discoveries are often tendentious:

> 'In 1968, there was no consensus that alcoholism was a medical disorder. Now some believe … that in addiction a person's brain is no longer able to produce … "free will." That's an oversimplification. Addiction is behavior: the persistent seeking and using of drugs despite negative consequences. … But a large majority quit voluntarily and permanently without treatment. … Addicts respond to incentives such as the sanctions employed by treatment programs in drug courts.' (85)

Is alcoholism a disease? Is it inherited genetically? Or is it simply a lack of personal responsibility? If we accept the genetic explanation, the drunk is immediately exonerated and his alleged helplessness is reinforced. If, on the other hand, drunkenness is due to poor discipline, it may be remedied by personal control. Many "studies" purport to show that boozing is genetic and therefore inherited.

Are these studies valid? It's hard to know, but keep in mind that many similar studies are products of confirmation bias and confuse correlation with causation. It is likely that, without empirical confirmation, many claiming a genetic cause are incorrect and that the origin of alcoholism remains unknown, except to say that it may be reversed by the drinker's will. "Discoveries" occur conveniently to explain and exonerate "victims" of social disorders. Almost on cue, new evidence is found which tends to support leftist ideology. Because, says the left, if all antisocial behavior is due to victimization, then (a) punishment is indefensible, (b) we need a much larger and more therapeutic government in order to rehabilitate them, and (c) large government is what socialism is all about. Psuedoscience tends to confirm the idea that government, with enough money, can solve all mankind's ills.

The Left has been at pains to show that America's black community is disadvantaged socially and economically because of white bias and discrimination and is incarcerated at high rates for the same reasons. To suggest that poor blacks (and whites) are the authors of their own impoverishment is to violate political coreectness:

"It is taboo to acknowledge that socioeconomic disparities between blacks and whites might be caused by intergroup differences in cultural values, family structure, interests, or abilities." (86)

Leftist science continues to insist that disparities must be explained by bias, explicit and implicit, and has enthusiastically endorsed an Implicit Association Test (IAT), which purportedly demonstrates prejudice even when hidden. Announcement by the scientific community that such a test was available prompted corporate and government leaders to fund anti-bias training for their employees, at great expense, only to find that (a) a person's test score can vary significantly each time he takes the test, undercutting its reliability as a psychological instrument, and (b) test scores have almost no connection to "discriminatory behavior". The authors of this test "now admit that the IAT does not predict 'biased behavior'". (ibid). And, contrary to political correctness, poor performance by blacks may be explained otherwise:

"...the large racial gap in academic skills (which) renders preposterous any expectation that blacks and whites would be proportionately represented in the workplace. and, vast differences in criminal offending are sufficient to explain racial disparities and incarceration rates." (ibid).

We continue to be misled by psueudoscience and the left's belief that renaming facilitates understanding, removes stigma, and replaces blame with compassion; calling it something else, they insist, may remove the disgrace. But further antisocial behavior may be encouraged by its renaming:

'The extension of the term "addiction," for example, to cover any undesirable but nonetheless gratifying behavior that is repeated is one example of the denial of personal agency that has swiftly percolated downward from academe. Not long after academic criminologists propounded the theory that recidivists were addicted to crime (bolstering their theories with impressive diagrams of neural circuits in the brain to prove it), a car thief … asked me for treatment of his addiction to stealing cars—failing receipt of which, of course, he felt morally justified in continuing to relieve car owners of their property.' (50)

Hear Goldberg "In other words, tell someone that his stealing is not really wrong, or … not his fault, … and he will be less likely to resist the temptation to steal"(80) The same can be said of alcoholism, drug addiction, and violent crime.

Unfortunately, the belief that murderers should be exonerated because of incompetent parenting extends to penal attitudes, and liberals hope to persuade us that harsh imprisonment is inhumane and counterproductive. Prisoners' civil rights are loudly defended by the American Civil Liberties Union, who insist that a welcoming environment, including personal comfort, entertainment, and the usual amenities, be available. So we've created an entirely pleasing environment that contradicts an earlier meaning of punishment. Many committed criminals look forward to imprisonment. It relieves them of the need to feed themselves, and, importantly, it augments their infamy and "street cred." The more frequent their incarceration, the more fearful their neighborhood reputations, which for many is the ultimate goal. It is absurd to maintain convicted murderers at great expense to the state while their unending appeals continue. Once paroled, their recidivist murders are the fault of those paroling, and those likely to recommit murder should be considered for early execution. Our penal system doesn't really punish very much, which no doubt contributes to our high crime rate.

Who benefits from classifying antisocial behavior as disease rather than bad habit? The rehabilitation industry (psychiatrists, psychologists, and sociologists) profits from that classification, since they purport to cure those "illnesses" and are reimbursed by the state for "intervening." This same industry says they can testify with certainty that (a) crime is a product of disease, and therefore criminals must receive prolonged psychiatric treatment rather than harsh punishment, and (b) those they have treated, including murderers, are now ready for parole and won't recidivate, certainly not violently. But in fact, murderers probably should never be paroled:

'It is obvious that a murderer in prison cannot commit another murder out of prison.' (80)

Shouldn't the psychological/psychiatric industry admit that they cannot predict who will and will not recidivate? Shouldn't they withhold parole from violent criminals, admitting their predictions of future behavior are unreliable? They should indeed, but to confess the inefficacy of 'intervevention' would cast doubt on the social sciences, which have become a fundament of the leftist therapeutic bureaucracy. We are urged, in the name of compassion, to welcome parolees to the larger community, and to give them jobs, despite knowing that many will recidivate.

Leftism and its compassionate disciples see minimum-wage legislation as a way to redistribute wealth, to arrive more nearly to the perfect egalitarian state. If inequity can be abolished, they believe, many social ills will disappear. And some 'studies' have tended to strengthen this liberal hope. Minimum- wage laws, in this thinking, will erase crime, and police will prove unnecessary. But, as Sowell reminds us, it was enacting a minimum-wage in 1930 that began the increase in black unemployment, and Detroit's decline. Those whose productivity cannot earn the new higher wage often lose their jobs:

'Minimum-wage laws are about as clear a case as one can find of a measure the effects of which are precisely the opposite of those intended by the men of good will who support it. Many proponents of (these laws) quite properly deplore extremely low rates; they regard them as a sign of poverty, and hope to reduce (it). In fact, insofar as minimum-wage laws have any effect at all, their effect is clearly to increase poverty. ... The effect of the minimum wage is therefore to make unemployment higher than it otherwise would be... The people who are rendered unemployed are precisely those who can least afford to give up the income they had been receiving, small as it may seem to (those) voting for the minimum wage.' (52)

The effort to display a conspicuous compassion toward the poor makes many of them poorer. 'States like California are ... creating labor-cost mandates that exceed the productivity of the employees to which they apply.' (87)

Ignoring this advice and experience to the contrary, the left won't stop trying; they will continue to urge an elevated wage, especially near elections, when the appearance of "compassion" for the poor raises their likelihood of reelection. This letter appeared in the Winston-Salem Journal:

"In 2015, the neighboring city of Greensboro passed a resolution to raise the minimum wage for city workers to $15/hr. ... Can't Winston-Salem recognize the worth of its workers and do the same?" (88)

Typically liberal, the letter is long on compassion and short on understanding. It favors city workers at the expense of customers and taxpayers, who are expected to make up the difference between current wages and the proposed new minimum; unwittingly, the writer is advocating fewer jobs, therefore lesser income, the very opposite of her stated intent. Her ill-informed compassion for the poor may in fact be injuring them.

V

Immigration

Current immigration policy in the United States is partly in response to the guilt generated by US slavery and the need to believe that bigotry and "otherism" have disappeared from American Life. In Western Europe, Hitler and his attempted genocide have generated similar guilt and an unrestrained attitude toward immigration. Hoping to expiate its historical sins (the Holocaust, slavery, Jim Crow, eugenics, Vichy anti-Semitism, colonial 'imperialism' the Western world now recounts past sinning and, as if in a Catholic confessional, proudly displays its efforts at penance. "Diversity" is redemptive, at least in lip-service:(while Academia preaches it, the faculties chosen are almost uniformly Liberal-Leftists).

'Now "diversity" has come to mean exploiting differences and using them as a cudgel to extract advantages based on national origin, skin color, or sexual preference. The problem with this kind of diversity is that it divides, pitting groups against each other. It's now an act of hostility, … stigmatizing anyone who doesn't confer privilege to the self-defined oppressed group. Diversity moves us away from MLK's dream of confraternity among different peoples and equal justice under the law.' (17)

Expressing guilt for past socio-cultural infractions has become one of the West's preoccupations. Much of its self-defeating immigration policy is explainable only as expiation for historical transgressions. The cultural and financial cost of importing millions of people with differing religions and cultures must be endured, we are told, as the correct and humane thing to do. The invasion of the United States by refugees from Mexico, Central America, and Islam must be tolerated, and protesting only confirms one's deplorability as racist, white supremacist, and "anti-other."

Used to be that immigration was carefully controlled: Immigrants in the late nineteenth and early twentieth century needed a sponsor in the United States and/or a job awaiting them. Knowledge of English and a bit of the US constitution were required, and disease resulted in either quarantine or deportation. Large immigrant groups in that period were almost exclusively

Judeo-Christian. But those limitations have either been removed or are now often unenforced. Counter-cultural immigrants are accepted in large numbers, encouraged by leftist Democrats (and some Republicans); most are unvetted, and those who entered illegally are encouraged to stay, issued drivers' licenses and welfare benefits (via their US-born children).Some will be permitted to vote. Admission of many Haitians with AIDS was urged by the Left in the 1970s, perhaps toseem sympathetic to and receive the votes of homosexuals and their vocal lobby. Introducing that disease en masse not only spread it to many US homosexuals and drug users but initiated a serious resurgence of tuberculosis, previously well contained. The Left insisted that it would be racist to exclude these disease-bearing immigrants.

The world, according to Douglas Murray (41) has been expiating for Germany's death camps since 1945:

> "The overwhelming German guilt has spread across the (European) continent and affected even our cultural cousins in America. ... We have fallen for the idea that we are uniquely guilty, uniquely to be punished, and uniquely in need of having our societies changed as a result."

Despite knowing that unvetted immigrants are prone to felony, we are informed by our leaders that violent crime among them is no greater than among our native population, and heartened to expect only four violent criminals per thousand immigrants. Ever larger numbers are encouraged despite their crime, and despite the antipathy of some to Christianity. The left hopes to see the US white population in the minority.Europe also has a left, whose impulse when confronted with massive immigration was to encourage still more. Compliant politicians seem to have believed that if the native population objected, it would largely be due to ethnic differences, not religious or cultural variations. But cultural differences soon proved troublesome, sometimes violent, and by then it was too late: "Parallel" unassimilated Islamic communities had already formed in larger cities in France, Belgium, and the Netherlands, and policing, while often required, was undertaken only timidly, partly for fear of Muslim violence and partly for fear of violating political correctness. Misunderstanding Islamic doctrine and its violent response to religious satire (e.g., *Charlie Hebdo*) was the fault of the European political class, who had denied that any real conflict existed between natives and Muslims.

Politicians, hoping to soften popular opposition to what had become an invasion, explained that birthrates remained low in Europe and the United States, and as the native population aged, foreign workers were needed to pay tax and sustain retirement pensions. So immigration must continue, to finance social welfare programs and to expiate our national guilt.

But guilt, atonement, and imported taxpayers have had severely adverse social effects. Uncontrolled immigration without language requirements weakens native cultures, and many immigrant Muslims remain hostile to Christians and Jews. Native European and American culture may not survive these invasions, as Richard Lamm warned: Cultural mixing, which the Left strongly encourages, can be quite deadly to the culture receiving the immigrants. The Left insists that requiring English is elitist, denying its cultural importance in the United States; Liberals think it reflects "white supremacy." Effective assimilation, which requires English, is thus further weakened, and native culture replaced with foreign ways. Our seeming inability to defend US language and culture is seen by some immigrants as weakness; some invert our flag in a show of contempt, which some anticipated:

'Fear is more likely to engender respect, whereas love or compassion is mre likely to be regarded as a contemptible sign of weakness'(1)

Uncontrolled immigration, as urged by leftists, weakens US culture and political unity, and Barack Obama's "fundamental transformation" is that much easier. If we can be persuaded that our culture is historically evil and that we are descendants of racists, rapists, and white supremacists, then America's founding myths are destroyed and can be replaced with an egalitarian and compassionate socialism. And the Left continues to urge ever larger immigrations, even when it has become clear that they are often detrimental:

'The repeated mantra was that these poor economic refugees only wanted to do work Americans wouldn't do; everyone failed to see the … costs that have become overwhelming. … In Orange County CAL, one can clearly see the costs of unregulated immigration. … Local food banks are overwhelmed and crimes of all types have increased. Once-beautiful cities like Santa Ana have become crime-ridden and dangerous, full of gang-members openly flouting their affiliations while plying their criminal enterprises.' 42

Most illegal immigrants are poorly educated and unskilled, and a study by the Federation for American Immigration Reform says it costs the United States a net of $113 billion each year for their support.' The law (when applied) restricts welfare payments to immigrants who have been here 5 years, but their children are eligible upon birth, the funds controlled and shared by their parents. (43)

'My wife was a public-health nurse and many of her patients were illegal immigrants who knowingly were gaming the system. They even made appointments from Mexico before they came here to get free healthcare at her clinic. They knew they would get free health care, free diapers, and schooling if they came here. We need to combine dreamer compassion with logic and the rule of law. If we reward bad behavior, we'll get more of it.' (44)

The United States seems a bit overanxious to welcome immigrants, even illegals, and to shower them with benefits; overresponding to their plight, as if they were more of Himmler's deathcamp victims:

'…the current regime of laws and norms … toward refugees was devised in the years after

WWII, with the Nazi mass violence fresh in memory. … Individuals with a well-founded fear of being persecuted were given … asylum. But it is not persecution which provokes millions to flee Syria or Afghanistan,…(but)… the chaos engendered by frail failing states. … Even those who do have a right to refuge, the authors argue, do not have a right to pick a country. They have a right to shelter, but not to maximal prosperity or comfort. … It is to the benefit of all … that refugees remain close to home whenever possible, since their countries will need them once hostilities end.' (45)

But the Left, in its conspicuous compassion, requires our acceptance of these refugees, and ignores the cultural and religious differences which threaten Unites States culture.

'We are asked to believe something incredible: that the American character is defined only by its unlimited acceptance of diversity. A defined American character—devotion to republican principles, republican virtue, the habits and manners of free citizens, self-reliance, would in that case be impermissibly exclusive.' (1)

Multiculturalism (MC) urges us to think globally, to accept all religious and cultural ideas as if they are interchangeable. We are to especially ignore that Islam, as understood by many of its adherents, is inimical to Christianity. Alternatively, the left seems to suggest that the new global society will avoid any fundamental cultural ideas. But:

'The idea that it is possible to base a society on No cultural or philosophical presuppositions at all Or, alternatively, that all such presuppositions may be Treated equally so that no choice has to be made between them Is absurd. Immigrants enrich—have enriched—our culture, But they do so by addition rather than by subtraction or Division.' (46)

Multiculturalism means support for multiple cultures or ethnic groups within a society and urging that immigrant cultures be continued without assimilation. This definition of MC expresses the leftist attitude toward uncontrolled immigration; to their discredit, many politicians here and abroad have supported the idea that disparate cultures must be encouraged, even in the face of conflict with Christians. They have defended Muslim immigrants despite their attacks on US citizens. Recently, a Muslim man killed eight and wounded twelve in NYC, and he was heard shouting, "Allahu Akbar." Instead of sympathy from the larger Muslim community, we were told that they feared an anti-Muslim backlash. Absurdly, political leaders tried to persuade that the attacker was probably another deranged American, not a terrorist. We also learned that mosque surveillance in NYC, which might have prevented the attack, had been suspended for fear of violating political correctness. The UK has similar problems:

A few years ago, it came to light that police in (Britain) had for decades systematically turned a blind eye to the mass sexual abuse of children—at least 1400 victims—by Muslim men. … From … this the terrorists surely draw a great deal of comfort. It gives them the impression of living in a weak society that will be easy to destroy, so that their [terrorist acts are not in the least pointless. (46)

As America loses its religion, its righteousness fades. Cultural relativism says that Christian principles are no more valid than Islamic ones: Who are we to judge Muslim behavior? Aggressive white men have enslaved entire populations and prosecuted barbaric wars, so how can we sit in judgment on them? They may be criminals, but aren't we all? goes this leftist line of thought. Europe also is losing its traditional values and is now subject to an elite and often progressive rule from Brussels. Islam, on the other hand, rather than weakening, seems expansile, zealous, and evangelical; the meaning and presence of Allah is quite real. Blasphemy, while satirized in the West, continues to have meaning in the middle-East, and reprisals for a perceived slight to their deity may include murder. As Christianity wanes in the West, so does the ability to defend itself in a cultural war. If Muslims see themselves as morally superior, and if Christianity continues to weaken in the United States, we're likely to lose the war. In decades past, America would have defended its culture and religion vigorously. Now, not so much.

The Left insists on expiating for Hitler's holocaust and demonstrating that the far Right is dead in Europe. Liberal-leftist politicians are doing this by opening Europe's doors to large numbers (1,000,000 in Germany?) of immigrants, mostly Muslims from the Middle East and North Africa. This mixing of Christian and Muslim cultures is hoped to demonstrate (a) that the cultures are quite miscible and (b) that diversity and Multiculturalism are alive and well in Europe and eugenics and Nazis are long gone. Trouble is that some Nazis are still there, and the coerced "diversity" is reviving a European far Right: 'Britain First', "founded in 2011 by veterans of neofascist groups … [is an] ultranationalist group," and it joins France's National Front and Germany's AFD (alternative for Deutschland, now the country's third largest party) in the far-Right resurrection. On September 1, 2018, Nazi protestors saluted Hitler in Chemnitz following the stabbing death of a german man by muslim immigrants

"They have modernized the old and marginal ideology of racism into a new doctrine of cultural protectionism … without consensus on the future identity of Europe's nation-states, the nativist backlash will lead to tit-for-tat terrorism, increased nationalism…." Trying to create a diverse Europe, liberal-leftist politicians have inadvertently reawakened the very Nazism they hoped was long dead." (47) (a far-right party is also now active in Italy, and Mussolini teeshirts are seen in Rome)

Even after 9/11, when Islam's animus toward the West became clear, our politicians continued to urge unvetted immigration from the Middle-East; they continued to do so after further Jihad attacks here, which begs the question: Do our politicians represent our interests or those of some other group? Why should PC and multiculturalism (MC) trump public safety? Why do our elites prefer "diversity" to safety for US citizens? Here are a few suggestions:

The US welfare state has weakened the need and urge to work, and since many low-paying, menial, and manual jobs remain unfilled, immigrants are essential. (To rephrase, the US welfare state has weakened the need to work, so we're importing labor.) Tax-paying immigrants will support a waning Social Security fund.

There are no doubt a few truly compassionate people who expiate America's historic guilt by urging sanctuary for the Syrian exodus.

The Democratic Party buys future votes from a dependent class of immigrants.

There are radical black legislators who aim to dilute the white majority with "people of color."

Political-chic: It has become fashionable among American and European elites to advance the immigrant cause; some politicians covet the applause of the EU and UN for opening US and European doors.

Our political elites have been trained by leftist academics, who resent the capitalist order and view traditional America as gun-toting, Bible-thumping "deplorables." They believe that we need instruction in MC, so as to erase our bigotry and sense of "otherness." Coercion may be required, and leftist dogma has it that exclusionary whites must accept diversity, a kind of sensitivity training by immersion. As Sniderman (2009)(48) points out, many politicians are no longer acting on our behalf; instead, they have become the agents of that dogma, anxious to be seen as part of the intellectual elitism which aspires to hegemony in Europe and America.

So the world seems now to divide itself into two groups on the matter of immigration and the great exodus from the Middle East. The first are liberal politicians who wish to import lots of cheap labor and reliable votes, at the same time atoning for the historical sins of their constituents. The second group forms the majority, the native, receiving populations who are expected to accept this imported culture without protest and pay the taxes which (a) subsidize the immigrants, thereby (b) providing the maintenance of an often oppositional Muslim culture (48). In the Netherlands, a separate school system is made available for Muslim immigrant children, and Sharia courts may be on the way.

'The belief in MC's abilities to soften the collision between Muslim immigrants and the receiving culture is a favorite leftist notion. All cultures, according to this view, are miscible, and we should proceed quickly toward globalizing a world in which all will be brothers and sisters and love will defeat all differences. Classical Liberalism, indeed, believes that transplanting US culture to the Middle East will create the best of all worlds, and we can start right here at home by mixing Islam and a waning Christianity.' (49)

Conservatives remain skeptical about this mixing and would prefer a more empirical approach, seeing how things go before flooding the United States with even more Islamists. But the Left insists that admitting large numbers of refugees must continue, if only to show that "otherness" has been defeated. One imagines a meeting of the West's elites somewhere in a well-guarded place distant from "parallel" Muslim neighborhoods: Angela Merkel, wishing to be recognized as a member of this distinguished group, announces that Germany, anxious to erase memories of Dachau and Zyklon-B gas, will receive a million or more from Syria and receives prolonged applause from leaders of the EU and UN. She then returns to her well-guarded and gated community in an armed, chauffered automobile.

There are serious cultural differences to be considered when immigration in large numbers is contemplated. Muslim men, for example, see women differently than does the West. We permit, even encourage, a generous display of female flesh; short shorts and bikinis hide very little, and the current fashion emphasizes breast cleavage. Sex is ubiquitous in the US, and Cable TV offers soft pornography daily. Muslim men, however, prefer their women largely hidden—it is said, to prevent public sexual arousal. When these men encounter our largely-uncovered females, who dress to excite, some are aroused to assault, even rape, as in Germany on New year's eve January 1, 2016. This should be ignored, says the Left, and we must proceed to full immersion of Islam in Western culture.

'The Netherlands, all agree, has been an exemplary case of immigrant multiculturalism. It has awarded special influence to minority community leaders, established a separate state-funded school system for minorities; funded and organized housing projects designed to accommodate their religious practices, dedicated a significant portion of radio and TV media broadcasting time to minority interests ... and ... increased the power of the spokesmen for the Muslim community, who pride themselves on rejecting Western European values.' (49)

In other words, Dutch politicians stressed separateness rather than assimilation and tolerance. In their effort to show that "otherness" died with eugenics and Nazis in 1945, leftist political leaders have inadvertently resurrected those very ideas and groups. Ironically, importing members of an opposing culture, and insisting that they be well-received and subsidized, may be the best way to assure resurgence of the radical Right in Europe; the leftist ruling elite wants multiculturalism, even if this is antithetical to native traditions.

'As Sniderman (48) points out, there are two models of politics: one is (1) bottom-up, in which representatives are democratically elected to act as voters' agents and are expected to respond to voters' needs; but there is increasing evidence that Western politics have become (2) top-down, and politicians, rather than our agents, are acting in their own interests, even when they conflict with the voters.'

'No one would suggest that the Netherlands government committed itself to a policy of MC because of pressure from below. It was quite the other way around. ... In the United States, for example, the striking feature of … affirmative action … has been precisely the continuing commitment of political elites to it in the face of obvious and extreme unpopularity in the electorate as a whole. (Ibid)'

Our Western politicians have urged immigration of people whose culture contradicts ours, and, having done it, they seem to be saying, (a) never mind, it was the compassionate thing to do, and (b) the obvious solution to cultural conflict is to import even more. They defend their policy by saying (1) our aging population needs replacing, (2) immigrant workers will pay into a waning Social Security fund, and (3) we must disprove any remnant of "otherness" among us. The real reason seems to be that the Left wants a poorly-educated, dependent population as a voting bloc advancing toward socialism.

As the West sees a rise of white nationalism and white supremacy, (including Mussolini teeshirts in Rome) in response to Muslim suicide bombers and truck-driving murderers, our politicians are surely to blame; they see themselves as part of the ruling leftist elite, erasing the last trace of Nazism and the KKK. The irony is that their coercive immigration policies have reawakened the political Far Right here and in Europe.

Governor Richard Lamm understood that, since many of our political class have been indoctrinated by Schumpeter's "intellectual class," and since many remain "hostile to the capitalist order," leftist subversion recommends multiculturalism, and Christianity is often less favored than, say, Islam:

"In the [British] prison, there was much more Islamic evangelism than Christian. I would find Qurans and Islamic pamphlets … but never Bibles or Christian pamphlets" (50)

The Birmingham airport has set aside a room for "wudu," the Muslim ablutions before prayer, no other religion is catered for in this fashion … so the impression is inevitably given that Islam … is … privileged. From all this (willful neglect of Muslim crime by British authorities), the (Islamic) terrorists surely draw a great deal of comfort. It gives them the impression of living in a weak society that will be easy to destroy. … They perceive ours as a candle-and-teddy bear society. … We kill, you light candles(ibid)

Once we are persuaded by our leftist elites that America's historic and ongoing victimization of blacks, poor whites, and Native Americans can only be redeemed by transforming to a socialist state, we will be expected to effect Lamm's plan for destroying America. A coercive multiculturalism is introduced, which is made to seem redemptive, atoning for what the left sees as US ethnocentrism and cultural xenophobia:

'African-Americans, Asian-Americans, Latinos, and Native Americans have been the victims of an intellectual and educational oppression that has characterized the culture and institutions of the United States and the European-American world for centuries … (with) a systematic bias toward European culture and its derivatives." (60)

Responding to the charge that the West is culturally xenophobic, Bork writes:

'Could the multicultural animus against European culture and its derivatives emerge more clearly than that?...Here we have a direct statement that European culture is harmful to nonwhite children',... and the left prescribes multiculturalism to remedy that harm.(20)

But Richard Lamm(61)underderstands the danger to the United States (and Europe) posed by multiculturalism:

'I have a secret plan to destroy America. If you believe, as many do, that America is too smug, o white bread, too self-satisfied, too rich, let's destroy America. Here's my plan

(a) Make the United States a bilingual/bicultural country. History shows that no nation can survive the … antagonism … of two competing languages and cultures.

(b) 'Invent "multiculturalism" and encourage immigrants to maintain their own culture; I would make it an article of belief that all cultures are equal, that no cultural differences are important. We can make the United States a "Hispanic Quebec" without much effort.

(c) I would make our fastest-growing demographic group the least educated and add a second underclass, unassimilated, uneducated, and antagonistic to our (native) population

(d) Encourage the large foundations and big business to give lots of money to these (MC) efforts; I would invest in ethnic identity and establish the cult of victimology.

(e) Promote divided loyalties; I would celebrate "diversity" and stress differences rather than commonalities.

(f) Then I would place all these subjects off-limits, make them taboo to talk about. I'd find a word similar to "heretic" [for those disagreeing with my plan, to] stop discussion and paralyze thinking.' (How about racist, homophobe, islamophobe, sexist? How about political correctness?)

Lamm quotes Toynbee: '...An autopsy of history would show that all great nations commit suicide' America's gradual suicide is much desired by the political Left and is by now well on its way. An enormous welfare state has been created, which, according to some, has unfunded liabilities exceeding $150 trillion. Bankruptcy or a ruinous hyperinflation seems inescapable.

Most of us who oppose illegal immigration find it simply too expensive. In the long run, we cannot afford to offer full support to those whose limited abilities make it unlikely that their earnings and future tax payments will repay such generosity. Welfare for illegal non-citizens is an anomaly constructed by leftist-Democratic politicians hoping for more dependent voters. Paul Sperry(62)has recorded the enormous expenditures (>$115 billion) for welfare shared by illegals, received by their US-born children.

VI

"Free" Medical Care and its Adverse Effects

'Every hospital in the country has been ordered to cancel all non-mergent surgery (for a month) … in an unprecedented step by National Health Service officials. The instructions … will result in around 50,000 operations being axed, following claims by senior doctors that patients were being treated in third world' conditions. … NHS medical director says to stop (admitting) all but the most urgent cases, closing outpatient clinics for weeks as well as cancelling … plannedoperations' (*Daily Telegraph* London 1/3/18)(63)

Among politicians, free medical care is a favorite campaign pledge; many have been elected on that promise. It sounds good, but (a) it isn't free, (b) the cost will finally mandate rationing and (c) the quality of care will finally erode due to overuse by patients and the reality of the budget.

'(There was)…a total national Medicaid expenditure of $566 billion in 2016. By 2025, the Centers for Medicare and Medicaid Services estimate that national Medicaid spending will reach $929 billion, an increase of 64 percent …(but)… Medicaid recipients have no better health outcomes than people with no insurance.'64)

Many primary-care providers won't see Medicaid patients because of low reimbursement rates, so emergency rooms have been inundated with patients. The wait to see a specialist can last months' (65)

Bringing costs under control requires rationing or restricted hospital admissions; it is rationing even when given another name. A case in point is the Hospital Readmissions Reduction program, which penalizes hospitals with above-average readmissions for Medicare programs … (this policy) resulted in about 5400 additional deaths per year … perhaps due to delaying readmissions beyond the federal limit of thirty days.' (66)

'"The Future that Doesn't Work" is a compilation which includes critiques of the British

National Health Service (NHS) and its "free" care. Rising costs meant that many foreign-born physicians were hired at lesser expense, and in some cases the language difference prevented satisfactory history-taking and advice-giving.' (67)

Current high-technology care is very expensive, and its use will be constrained by attempts to restrain costs. Rationing and cost restraints in Canada have encouraged many there to seek care in the United States. One problem of 'free care' is its overuse; people who pay small fees or nothing to see a physician may visit him several times a week with only minor complaints. Finally the cost exceeds funding, and governments are forced to ration, which may take unusual forms:

'Britain's National Health Service (proposes) to ban patients from surgery indefinitely unless they lose weight or quit smoking. Studies in the United States have shown surgery in the morbidly obese and smoker groups have worse outcomes. On the administrative (funding) side, instituting such a plan would decrease total patients in surgical queue, improving statistics. However, this is only one of NHS's problems. ... The statistics show that 3.78 million patients are now waiting for NHS treatment—a rise of more than 50 percent since 2012. ... Royal College of Surgeons said: Too many patients are waiting excessively long for surgery and our concern is we will only see the situation worsen as impact of NHS ... decision to deprioritize the 18-week waiting time takes hold. The plan to delay surgery for smokers and the obese ... won't fix funding, understaffing, and delays in other areas of care.' (68)

Who will be deemed culpable if the patient who is obese or a smoker expires during the waiting interim? (69)

Despite the enormous cost predicted by the British experience, California is apparently proceeding with plans for universal single-payer health care. Jumping on the socialist train, Senator Sanders and other democrats are adding universal care to their platform. But, here's the rub:

'(...California's single payer medical care proposal is a) ... great idea, except you don't have to be a genius to predict there will be an Exodus of taxpayers from California and a flood of people from other states and countries into California. Of course, there will not be enough doctors who are willing to care for everyone who is seeking this free care.' (70)

For now, at least, Washington can borrow money to pay its share of the Medicaid tab, but states can't do that. State legislatures, trying to meet their ever-expanding Medicaid obligations, are instead cutting funding for schools, roads, and police. (64)'The enormous cost of "free" medical care is conveniently ignored as the politician lures voters by offering new benefits. It all sounds so utopian, and many are persuaded that it can be done by taxing just the rich, but that isn't so;

in California, a single-payer system will require (a) $225 billion from taxes paid to the federal government, and imposing (b) a 15% percent payroll tax, and … (c) likely a 31 percent increase in sales tax, plus (d) higher income tax … there is nothing free about this at all.' (71)

Democrats are proposing…'a single-payer healthcare system in which all private healthcare plans would be eliminated, and the available procedures limited…(and support) a medicare-for-all healthcare system that would cost $32 trillion, hike taxes, and nearly double the national debt.' (72)

Harry Truman settled a strike with coal-miners by offering them health insurance. Little did he know what complexity he was creating for future generations. Subsequently, health insurance was routinely included in many workers' contracts, and finally healthcare became, in leftist minds, a civil right. Private fee-paying gradually diminished as business-owners offered care as part of employee reimbursement. State and federal employees, and their families were included in "health insurance" plans. In private care, one of the factors controlling fees is the physician's need to face the patient he charges; it is difficult to justify high fees to ill and poor patients. But when the anonymity of third-party payment intervenes, no justification seems needed. And as insurance companies often pay a stated percentage of the doctor's submitted fee, there is every reason to inflate charges. Medical insurance tends, by its very nature, to make care more expensive. One way to reduce costs would be to return gradually to direct charging of the patient for care by the physician:

'A free market exists in one aspect of health care: laser eye surgery. It's generally not covered by insurance, so providers have to compete on quality and cost. The cost of laser surgery has dropped from $2200 per eye 20 years ago to $250 per eye today…'. (73)

The bureaucratization of Medicare and Medicaid means the office physician must deal with governmental insurance directives. He often needs to justify his procedures and charges to a distant administrator who has little sympathy for or understanding of the doctor's problems. Recently, new rules require extensive record-keeping, and doctors now complain that they spend more time talking to their computers than their patients. Many well-motivated doctors are offended by the interposition of the federal government and its bureaucracy between them and their patients:

'…meanwhile, the interests of patients (which used to be the main driver of medical care) have been replaced by concern for the bottom line. And physicians, who used to be the substance of medical care, now find themselves no more than compliant (and replaceable) cogs in the machinery…Becoming a physician no longer has the appeal of joining a profession in which one can expect to do a lot of good in the world…and earn a better-than-average living. If those are your aims, you would do better as a funeral director…(there is)… overinvolvement of government in medical care, when it should be doing more to promote good health…Fewer young people are entering the medical profession…there is a projected shortage of 42,000 to 121,000 physicians by 2030…' (74)

And, even after providing very expensive medical care for little payment, physicians, administrators, and even politicians must be chagrined to find that patients remain unsatisfied. Knee replacement, which was not possible until a few years ago, can restore a full life to those in severe pain. It is now available thanks to Medicare funding by taxpayers, but complaints continue:

'When I had my knee replaced, the billing from the hospital to my insurance company totaled $142,946. The insurance paid…(only)…$15,648' CoulieD WSJ ltrs 8/28/18

'…a charitable, nonprofit raises its prices…(and)…ultimately ends up with a 400% markup…(for)…knee replacement. The trustees should be embarrassed. The regulators should be investigating. The legislatures should be acting'. HettingerB(ibid)

There is no end to human wanting. Once life-extending surgery is made available, the electorate will increasingly expect it to be delivered completely free of charge.

VII

Women, Feminism, and the Left

'Nature has given women so much powerthat the law has very wisely given them very little'.

—Dr. Samuel Johnson

Women control sexual relations and nurture our children, and it would be foolish to suggest that they lack socialpower. Nonetheless, some of them insist that they are oppressed, and wish to replace the traditional patriarchy with an absurd and unrealistic gender egalitarianism.The advances of technology have freed women from their most arduous traditional tasks. Washing clothes, squeezing them dry, hanging them, adding large ice blocks to an icebox—these are no longer necessary. Freed from these daily tasks, they are intent on reminding us (and themselves) of their ongoing 'oppression' and subjugation by men. The contraceptive pill permits sexual freedom without pregnancy, another burden lifted. And yet, this newfound liberty only serves to recall for them how historically disadvantaged they have been; their alleged subjugation by men attracts the left, who persuade women that they are indeed 'victims' and see them as a reliable voting bloc. Liberal politicians see that by manipulating women's sense of exploitation, promising to remove its causes, and ennobling their social status, they may create a dependable source of political support. Surely, femininity is women's most precious asset, and has controlled the rise and fall of kingdoms; absurdly, some now are anxious to renounce femininity in favor of bigger biceps and more pushups.

With the assistance of the political Left, the feminist movement in America has grown increasingly aggressive. Ignoring the obvious advantages of womanhood, feminism insists on displaying male-female equivalence and says that the physical advantages of being male (strength, body size) are a "social construct," the result of habitually believing men are, say, stronger, and believing women are "softer". They suggest that restricting females to housework for centuries has resulted in a smaller, weaker body. Radical feminists insist that the only true difference between men and women is genitalia. The need to believe that women are physically equal includes the idea of "patriarchal bias," according to which females have been coerced into procreation, child-bearing, and child-rearing. Women are now minor partners, they say, in a male-dominated paradigm for living.

The absurd feminist concern for physical equality with men has become obsessive. In order to demonstrate it, women have insisted on being included in occupations previously restricted to males. Political pressure from the feminist movement has succeeded in creating female firemen, police detectives, and marines. But accomplishing this required lowering standards; the number of pull-ups, pushups, and miles run has had to be adjusted down to accommodate feminist theory. Lower standards may mean higher risk in dangerous jobs. Never mind-- says the Left-- social engineering is needed to prove our point. Hollywood supports feminist narratives, and most police dramas are now at pains to include at least one female detective, often as a superintendent.

Inclusion of women in the military, and especially the insistence that they occupy barracks with males, has met resistance from high-ranking officers. They point out that (a) men fight best while bonding as a unit, and (b) the introduction of females introduces sexual chemistry, competition for female attention, and often dis-bonding. Male unity is eroded by competitive behavior intended to attract the opposite sex, and, far from bonding, males begin to resent their competitors. Feminists insist that these problems are small and will dissipate once inclusion of women has become routine. So the need to establish equality with men has placed men at risk by lowering standards of employment and occupation.

'Even the military has apparently succumbed to the fashionable idea that there are no differences between the sexes, ... why must we pretend that men and women are the same or that masculinity is the problem? ... A society that won't let boys be boys willpay a price in the end.' (89)

As feminism intends to weaken the tradiitional patriarchy, it alienates women from potential mates, and encourages life without marriage. Without a husband's earnings, some single women hope to receive federal/state welfare benefits, and the left finds more dependent voters:

'Single women ... seem to want the financial security of marriage without the baggage of a husband and expect Washingtonto provide that support.' (90)

Feminists seem to believe that elevating women requires deconstructing men and demeaning maleness. In what seems to be punishment for historical 'oppression' of women, it has become common to see men portrayed as foolish and incompetent; TV ads routinely depict them as needing assistance from more intelligent females.The leftist campaign to elevate women has resulted in the deconstruction of maleness. Paradigms of masculinity that had guided generations of American boys are now thought to be excessively aggressive, and finally ridiculous. Women, it now seems, dislike traditional maleness, which is now denigrated as "macho", and prefer more passive males. The "metrosexual" is more likely to be welcomed to female company.

"There are virtually no positive male role-models left atall" (91)

'The left, securing feminist votes, has engineered the most remarkable event in human history—the end of patriarchy—within the space of a generation, a social system that has endured in every corner of the globe throughout recorded history had more or less crumbled.' (92)

Leftism has successfully included '…the arguments of race, social class, gender identity, homosexual oppression, transgender rights, and economic rights … within the framework of Feminism and…in an attempt to become relevant and convince more of their righteous zeal, the history of feminism marches on.' (93)

And feminism's subversion of centuries of European and American tradition corrodes Western culture, increasing its vulnerability to the socialist revolution. American children thought for decades that aggressive males like those celebrated in war- and western-movies should inform their adult lives; that there were heroic deeds that needed to be done, and those doing them would be admired by the girl-next-door. Instead, they now fiound that the aggressive model has become ridiculous, even offensive to women. Worse, it now seemed that men and masculinity were held in dislike, even contempt for their native aggressiveness. Young men who had thought to deal with the world's enemies by asserting their masculinity now received ridicule rather than adulation. How should our future national leaders behave, when passivity, softness, and frankly feminine virtues were now preferred, and men were demeaned?

At (Barnard College), where acknowledging intersectionality is de rigueur, one would expect to encounter dialogue about issues that men face too. However, after two years here, I have never witnessed students or professors broach the topic in a positive way. What's more alarming is how often female peers display conspiratorial glee when they make fun of and delegitimize men's issues'. (94)

The need to denigrate men has inevitably affected flirting and courtship. Feminism has created lots of female shoulder chips, and some women insist on collecting slights never intended. So men approaching women have become aware of the need to do so very carefully. Interaction previously considered acceptable has now become risky; one is reproached for, say, opening a car- door, and remarks such as 'nice dress' may be perceived as sexual harassment. Many women now see flirtation as offensive and insist that traditional attitudes toward them are unacceptable. Some of us thought that women dressed hoping to attract male attention, but the current #MeToo movement included women who found benign glances threatening. Men who are unwilling to accept this new standard have lost careers and fortunes following lawsuits for sexual harassment.

"'Sexism" is a pejorative, and seems to refer to any male behavior which reminds women of 'subjugation' and their former roles as nurturers and home-keepers. Flirting has become offensive to women; it reminds of traditional roles now eschewed by females, and it recalls patriarchy and suggests male superiority. Any sexual encounter must be approached with extreme caution by men, who are at risk, especially on college campuses, of becoming sexual predators, following even consensual sex. A young woman finds herself replaced in her boyfriend's affections after sex, accuses him of rape, and sees his academic and career futures ruined. Title IX, originally intended to include women in college athletics, has been extended by President Obama's administration to protect them in cases of alleged campus rape:

"David" and "Nancy" agreed to stay the night in his dorm room and to a sexual encounter. Oral sex was preferred to avoid pregnancy and was accomplished. Two days later, "Nancy" found that "David," who she thought would be eternally grateful for her sexual favors, ignored her, preferring another girl. Outraged, "Nancy" complained that she had been forcibly sodomized by "David" and lodged this complaint with the college administration. Since the broadening of Title IX, David is now at a serious disadvantage on many campuses: He can no longer insist on facing his accuser, and the usual presumption of innocence has been suspended. Nancy is presumed truthful and need not face David in accusation. David and Nancy are fictional, but similar couples and events are increasingly common on US campuses. Liberal- Democrats have come to see themselves as protectors of America's young and innocent females, and pandering to their fears on campus is hoped to result in votes from the feminist lobby.

'In 2011 the Education Department's Office of Civil Rights construed Title IX, which bars sex discrimination, as mandating that colleges and universities take a series of actions meant to prevent and punish "the sexual harassment of students, including sexual violence." Campus administrators set up disciplinary tribunals that lack basic due-process protections for the accused. Candice Jackson … acting head of the Office of Civil Rights, told the *NY Times* in July that '…"the accusations--90 percent of them--fall into the category of 'we were both drunk' … we broke up, and six months later I found myself under a Title IX investigation because she just decided that our last sleeping together was not quite right." (95)

Protecting the accuser has meant putting the accused at risk of losing graduate school acceptances and perhaps gaining jail time. So a young woman, angry after conferring her highest favor, can now seriously punish last night's lover just because his attentions lie elsewhere. Feminism has created antagonists of men and women who once would have been less contentious. And the sexual revolution has encouraged an attitude which denigrates sex:

'The sexual revolution promised freedom but delivered bondage to millions who believed the lie that human sexuality is little more than a bodily function. In the process, both men and women have been degraded and dehumanized. We have believed the unbelievable (feminist) lie that men and women are the same. We have exchanged the truth for a lie.' (96)

A bikini was once defined as two spangles and a Band-aid. The current dress code for young US females is less revealing but sometimes not by much. Bras that augment by squeezing and peek-a-boo skirts barely concealing skimpy underwear are now quite common. Some will consider this dress code as an invitation to sex, but beware: the game seems to be 'look but don't touch," and an eager male response may be seen as harassment. Men deemed guilty may lose careers and worse. Many prominent male radio and TV personalities have recently lost jobs, money, and reputations by accusations of persistent, unwanted attentions. Some long-standing TV hosts have been replaced, their programs now hosted by mostly females.

In many ways, flirting and courtship have become quite difficult. If the male is too passive, he is unlikely to achieve his ultimate goal; if too aggressive, he is likely to be spurned as "sexist" and hypermasculine, perhaps accused of sexual assault.(One wonders if the apparent increased incidence of homosexuality in the United States might be an alternative to unwelcome women). Young males in particular are, in feminist America, likely to think of themselves as unworthy; they are discouraged for being too physical, too aggressive, too rough. Many traditional ways of expressing masculinity are now avoided, because they are seen as either hazardous (dodgeball?) or overly competitive, rewarding only those who are adept, ignoring those who are not. Rather than encouraging the most athletic to excel, some now see athletic competitions as unfair to the non-athlete, giving rise to feelings of inadequacy. The liberal-left's obsession with equality is violated when only a few can hit home-runs, and football, once the acme of US masculinity, may soon be softened or discontinued. Manliness, then, is passe', and courting is hazardous:

'Until revised rules take effect, my clear advice to college men of today is don't date women from the college you attend. Don't so much as share a table with them in the campus cafeteria, don't talk to them on the way to or from classes, and don't, by all means, do anything aggressive like high-fiving them after a touchdown at the Saturday football game. Don't speak to them, don't communicate with your eyes, don't hold a door open for them. Anything you do or say can be held against you. Any touching could begin the near-irreversible end of your academic career. Pour wax in your ears if you must.' (97)

The contraceptive pill and ensuing sexual revolution were seen as introducing a new freedom to young men and women, who could now vent sexual pressure freely without fear of reproducing. Feminists everywhere saw this as an opportunity to avoid marriage, thus avoiding male oppression. But it also encouraged multiple partners and weakened allegiance to marriage. If one's spouse wasn't as satisfying as Hollywood led us to expect, one might as well sleep with someone else; nothing sacrosanct about marriage, after all. Inevitably, the number of second (and third) marriages increased, and the commitment to any one person began to seem old fashioned, out of date, anachronistic. Many children became poorly defined parts of an

'..."extended" family, some of whom are now issuing "primal screams" at political rallies, asking"Who am I"'(98)

VIII

Affluence, Guilt, and America's New Religion

'An idle mind is the devil's workshop' anonymous

Those of us born during the Great Depression (1929–41?) thought our mission was to become affluent. Wasn't that America's raison d'être and its ultimate goal? Some of us had endured cramped quarters and shared bathrooms with other families during the post-WWII housing shortage, and hoped to escape that unpleasantness. We wanted our own homes, lots of cars, radios, and TVs, and we assumed that others wanted the same. We were not just keeping up with the Joneses. We hoped to pass them on the way to affluence.

At least since the end of World War II, America has concentrated on making us all richer. Families worked toward and yearned for the material success that would make life easier and elevate them to a new, wealthier class. We are, most of us, much richer. US real GDP per capita in 1947 was $1,347; in 2017, it was $52,347.96. So much wealth has been generated in seventy years that the number of automobiles, estimated at 6 million in 1930, now exceeds 247 million. In 1945, there were likely fewer than ten thousand TVs in US homes; now there are 217 million. Basic needs seem to be available for everyone. Ask, and even in God's absence, the government will see that you receive.

Suppose now that, after all that striving, affluence is weakening the allegiance Americans feel toward capitalism, the very order that provided their wealth. And suppose that the United States we've known is unraveling, due at least in part to its wealth:

'Nowadays the young act as the spoiled children of the rich. We are discovering that there is such a thing as an "ordeal of affluence", that diffused affluence subjects the social order to greater strain and threatens social stability more than does diffused poverty. Order and discipline have up to now been attributes generated in the battle against want … absence of want and work create a climate of disintegrating values with its fallout of anarchy. … Both the children of the well-to-do

49

and of families on welfare don't need to share in the world's work. ... Crime in the streets and insolence on campus are sick forms of adolescent self-assertion... Until recently, scarcity, the factory, long working-hours, etc, tamed and disciplined people automatically. Now, with affluence and leisure, people are no longer kept in line by circumstances...' (18), and the proverbial fear of "shirtsleeves to shirtsleeves in three generations" has again become pertinent.

So, something happened on the way to affluence. Some say that human beings are at their best when slightly hungry, when they are more likely to need religion and work. Dispelling the fear of want requires discipline and creates a sense of purpose. As Emerson reminds us "Each man's task is his life-preserver." But as a diffused affluence develops, the need for religion and work diminishes, and life loses purpose. Many become overfed and lazy, committing themselves to a life of cola, potato chips, and a couch from which to watch a never-ending series of banal TV dramas. The discipline needed for steady work diminishes, and existence for many becomes a lifelong loaf. The destructive effects of affluence will seem paradoxical to many; our wealth permits us to quit work, to sleep and play as we desire, without financial obligation. This is why we worked, only now to find that we may be undone by it. A loss of meaning, a failing sense of purpose, and the waning of religious belief make many vulnerable to leftist utopian promises. For some, the utopian urge to dispel all social inequity replaces task and meaning in life, and takes on a religious commitment to resolve every perceived unfairness. Forgetting that the present social order represents many centuries of evolved adaptation to group living, and that 'there's a reason things are the way they are', leftism wishes to dismantle a well-functioning Western civilization.

Irony of ironies: the very capitalist system that brought our citizens affluence and material wealth beyond their dreams is now seen by many as greedy, exploitive, excessively competitive, and inequitable. The cultural decay brought on by affluence is not without historical precedent. Hear Polybius writing in the second century BCE:

> 'The handing down of privileges to future generations is done without the latter understanding the discipline that was needed to create those privileges ... As soon as a new generation has succeeded and the democracy falls into the hands of the grandchildren of its founders, they have become by this time so accustomed to privilege that they cease to value it, and the most liable to this temptation are the rich...'(19)

Bork (1996) writes,'Men are kept from rootless hedonism ... by religion, morality, and law ... and the necessity for hard work, ... usually physical, and the fear of want. These constraints were progressively undermined by rising affluence in America ... Affluence brings with it boredom ... A life centered on consumption will be devoid of meaningReligion, morality, and law tend tobe strongest when life is hard. ... When life is easy, ... modern religion eschews proscriptions and commandments and turns to counseling and therapeutic sermons, relative morality and law, especially criminal law, become soft and uncertain. The very affluence that was sought so diligently tends to weaken the social order which provided it...' (20)

> 'The problems facing the US originate from a generation of affluent youth growing up in the 1960s and 70s who weakened unique American institutions and values that their hard-working parents created, ... giving rise to policies which encouraged dependency on the government and weakened the family. Subsequent generations inherit the privileges of democracy without effort and cease to grasp and cherish what brought those privileges. Venally ambitious politicians arise and promise comforts to the masses, who vote but misperceive that the bribes benefits for votes didn't cost them a thing. Civic cohesion weakens and mob-rules and violence starts. ... Affluence brought weakened discipline ... Without national military serviceyoung people demanded "rights without obligations." '(21)

America was once quite religious, even evangelistic, trying to sell its religion and culture to other peoples. Capitalism and the Christian God were thought by many to be quintessentially American, and this gospel was urged worldwide. But Christianity in the United States is eroding; one estimate is that only 15% of its citizens regularly attend church. As it weakens, so does a sense of rightness, correctness, and moral rectitude; many are no longer sure that God exists or that capitalism is good, so how can America seem so righteous?

Blasphemy means: irreverence towards anything regarded as sacred; cursing or reviling God; indignity offered to God in words or writing. I define it because the word is now infrequently heard, and may not be understood. It was once a serious offense among us; blasphemers were sinners. Now the word is rarely heard, even when the Christian God is blasphemed. 'The Book of Mormon' thrives on blasphemous humor, and plays nightly to large audiences. The Christian God is now rarely defended, and neither is Western Christian culture. Western Europeans have welcomed large numbers of Muslim immigrants whose culture is antithetical to their own, arriving daily on their southern beaches. Far from defending their culture from this invasion, their politicians urge them to receive these immigrants willingly. Are they atoning, perhaps for Holocaust sins? The immigrants must be greeted warmly, politicians advise, because their misery provokes a compassion which the West is anxious to display. And as Western culture is displaced by this incursion, native Westerners seem to be saying that their own culture isn't worth defending, and are surprised to see that anyone, even a Muslim, would bother to defend their God, much less behead a blasphemer. The guilt of slavery, genocide, and 'otherism' is compounded by the guilt of those who find their wealth unearned, therefore sinful, requiring an exaggerated compassion for the less advantaged.

To review briefly: Polybius and others believed in historical cycles and evolving forms of government; they thought that monarchy fades to aristocracy, which finally becomes democracy; democracy weakens to become anarchy, and then, restoring order, to despotism. Some think our democracy shows signs of weakening and see early evidence of anarchy. Cities in California and New York declare themselves "sanctuaries" independent of US law with regard to immigrants. In Berkeley, students confusing freedom of speech with freedom to burn, have ignited university buildings without apparent punishment; the police, told by community leaders to "stand-down," watch the burning without responding. President Trump has issued executive orders limiting immigration for some Muslims, but those orders are ignored in several US communities, and liberal-leftist courts have issued injunctions against the orders. Are we nascent anarchists? Is there a growing contempt for the law in America? Will more neighborhoods be unsafe? Has the promise of liberty been misunderstood and oversold?

One of America's familiar rallying cries is "Freedom," a rhetorical theme that politicians repeat ad nauseam without explaining its limitations in a social context. "Life, liberty, and the pursuit, etc." are incantations oft-repeated, and finally persuade many Americans that behavioral proscriptions of any kind are unconstitutional. The need for civil order, they believe, violates their right to conduct their lives as they wish. In this sense, Americans have been overpromised and misled once again by politicians, and their misunderstanding of liberty's limitations encourages social, moral, and finally political anarchy.

'Intellectuals have played a big role in shaping arguments for loosening the traditions of self-restraint … The sense of the sacred and the shameful gradually declined across the twentieth century … Writers and artists demanded that the traditional union of moral and aesthetic judgment be dissolved. … The result … was a culture's slow but steady estrangement from any coherent moral tradition.'(22)

As affluence weakens social and moral bonds, and people forget how their parents arrived at wealth, we are in danger of discarding not just capitalism but Christianity. As the need to work is ended by rising affluence, religion is also weakened. People need God when facing adversity, but when affluent, not so much. When things are going well, God and Church seem increasingly less important, even slightly irritating, and we begin to believe we don't need them. American evangelism was once at pains to persuade our less fortunate world partners that Christianity and material wealth go together; Calvin taught that hard work and high earning identified one as among God's chosen. But the need tio believe that Christianity and hard work will bring us all to happiness fades as affluence arrives. And the need to defend Christianity and its God declines.

An idle mind may indeed become the Devil's workshop, and affluence creates idle minds and bodies. When confronted with capitalism's inequities, our affluent youth insist that (a) a compassionate government must restore equity, and (b)socialism must be the long-term answer for our continuing disparity in earnings. The left is elated to find that young people are anxious to voice their compassion for the disadvantaged and find that they are vulnerable to socialist indoctrination. This is because the young often can't see the connection between their material wealth and the capitalist order. Not working, they don't understand the relationship between work and wealth; not having been without material wealth, they can't conceive its absence and don't see why simply redistributing wealth can't solve economic disparity. When it is explained to them that socialist redistribution has always failed, that coercion is required to establish it, and that 100 million deaths in the twentieth century are attributed to its implementation, they'd rather not believe it.

They continue to believe in the beauty of the socialist ideal, From him who has to him who needs, and think that previous attempts to realize the ideal were poorly done, and can now be avoided. This next time, learning from Lenin's, Stalin's, Mao's, and Castro's errors, they will create paradise under a collectivist regime. Historically collectivism has failed because of a failure to agree on the definition of utopia.But leftism and our youth convince themselves that they can correct previous errors and succeed where Lenin failed.

Many in my generation thought that material wealth should be our goal; we should eventually exceed materially our parents and grandparents. That would be, they thought, the pinnacle of our civilization, America's reason for being. God's blessings seemed to be confirmed by our rising wealth. But now that affluence had arrived, religion seemed less important, and Sunday sermons became a bore. Cadillacs and summer homes replaced piety, churchgoing, and fervent prayer. God became increasingly irrelevant, and the need for an afterlife dissolved when artificial knees and hips suggested that they might live forever. But then it slowly became clear that happiness wasn't entirely achievable by material comfort alone. They had forgotten how work had defined their reason for being, and how Churches had been able to define life's meaning in transcendental terms.

"We have drifted far from our inheritance as the children of pioneers to fashion a culture that teaches its young to love too much the privileges and protections of wealth(23)

Americans used to be orderly, disciplined, and well-motivated to work. Diffused affluence has changed many of us. We have become lazy, overfed, and without purpose. We were happier when we each had a task to perform to house and feed ourselves.Many of us now want only leisure, high-tech entertainment, and drugs. Overfed and thinly educated, we are seen by the left as susceptible to egalitarian and collectivist rhetoric, which exploits our gullibility, and further weakens our allegiance to Republican government and a capitalist economy. Americans now insist on being dulled by stale television 24/7, and many see drugs as providing the only real happiness. Politicians will deliver enough benefits to keep America happy, in return for electoral support. They will work to increase the size of a dependent population through unvetted immigration and inflation of the welfare state, ensuring ever more voters and continued reelection. This is the unwritten, tacit contract between citizen and legislator. God, meanwhile, is not only irrelevant, but slightly distasteful.

'Progressive (leftists) simply cannot contain their distaste toward symbols and beliefs important to ordinary Americans. … Those denouncing … offers of prayers (for those murdered at the First Baptist Church in Texas) don't really want an argument. They want to express their feelings of moral superiority.' (24)

In 1789 France, those favoring the end of the monarchy and urging a Republic also wanted to end religion. Historically, Churches have often been attacked by political leaders because (a) allegiance to faith detracts from the government's power, and (b) the money generated by them as tithing, gifts, and legacies is much desired by the same government. Further, Churches are sometimes wealthy landowners; Henry VIII made sure to confiscate valuable property in England following his break with the Roman Church. The Soviet state did its best to weaken the Orthodox Christian Church, in part because they wanted to replace God with state. Christianity has been waning for decades in the United States. But never fear, the Left offers a replacement; a progressive secularism may soon replace Christianity as America's church of choice.

'The public mind has by now so thoroughly grown out of humor with (capitalism) as to make its condemnation a foregone conclusion…New social religions will always have that effect…in 300 AD it would not have been easy to expound the achievements of ancient civilization to a fervent believer in Cnristianity…the most obvious misstatements… are applauded…' (8)

New and vibrant religions, one assumes, are more than just a church building and a Sunday sermon; commitment, devotion, and zeal characterize a fresh faith. Liberal Leftism, and its commitment to a collective, redistributionist, egalitarian statism, promote a zeal reminiscent of religious faith. A new catechism includes political correctness, as well as definitions of other prescribed and proscribed behaviors. Just as Christianity controlled its adherents with accusations of 'original sin', leftism now insists that slavery, jim-crow, and ongoing bias are sins which require redemption. The Republican center-right, by definition, contains serious sinners, presumptively guilty of violating political correctness, and lacking conspicuous compassion:

'Today, any Republican charged or implicated with racism-- however tendentious, outrageous, implausible, exaggerated, or false the charge—will quickly surrender, often preemptively. This applies equally to other violations of political-correctness: homophobia, Islamophobia, xenophobia, sexism, and a host of other so-called irrational prejudices. After all, there is no rational defense against an 'irrational fear', which presumably is what the phobias are. Republicans have rendered themselves defenseless against PC…Only President Trump seems undeterred by the tyrannous threat that rests at the core of PC.'(1)

The Left has proclaimed the need for redemption. Insisting that our founding fathers were corrupted by slavery, and that the nation's founding remains therefore immoral, we'll be told that expiation is required: displaying a conspicuous compassion for our oppressed fellow-Americans will be one route to expiation. And, as in pre-Luther Catholicism, dispensations may be purchased, this time by ever-larger taxes to the central government

When America still believed in God and Church, it saw itself as morally upright and virtuous, usually convinced that its course was just. But as devotion to God has diminished, so has a sense of righteousness, which is now often seen as hypocritical sanctimony. Coupled with multiculturalism, which insists that all cultures are equivalent, we no longer believe in our exceptionalism, and are increasingly vulnerable to cultural and religious invasions. It has become unacceptable to censure foreign religions, which now smacks of bigotry and violates political correctness. Islamists often wish us ill, but we are urged by a leftist elite to overlook their hostility and work towards an imminent global brotherhood. It would be "extremist," we are told, to believe that (1) that God and Allah are incompatible and (2) that Islam is a Trojan horse, offering peace but delivering terror.

Once we might have distrusted and rejected Islam and its practitioners as antithetical and inimical to Western Christianity. As currently understood by many of its adherents, Islam instructs in a zealous righteousness which allows only one religion. It may well be that well-educated, upper-class Muslims understand and accept multiculturalism, but many of those entering Western Europe and America seem to be proletarian; manual laborers, they are less educated, and religiously and culturally immiscible. But as Christianity wanes in the West, our sense of righteousness fades, and we are unable to respond to the dangers of mass immigration by the followers of a jealous Allah. Political correctness permitted the Fort Hood massacre; those who anticipated terror were prevented from speaking by fear of seeming anti-immigrant. PC also prevents adequate surveillance of US mosques.

'Communism (and socialism) are religions, and like other religions, they have their own morality, ethics, and history of slaughtering perceived heretics, nonbelievers, and enemies of the "faith." It is not the first religion to have killed millions of people.' (25)

The liberal- left's priesthood is in academia, Washington, and Hollywood, and fills liberal newspapers. It doesn't need churches or much infrastructure. Sunday sermons are New York Times editorials. Those of us who express surprise that a small number of leftists have successfully propagated a new religious belief should remember that Christ had only 12 disciples:

'…21st century progressivism is also a religion—a militant faith, a true church in nearly all important respects. It is a community of belief and shared values, with dogmas, heresies, sacraments and fanatics; with saints it reveres and devils it abhors, starting with the great satan Donald Trump. If religion were to disqualify a catholic from public service, it would logically have to disqualify a practicing progressive, who is the creature of a belief system that is, on the whole, considerably more dogmatic than the one with headquarters in Rome.' (107)

Like other religions, leftism offers an improved way of living, a series of pre- and proscriptions, which, if followed, purport to lead to ultimate happiness. The usual Ten Commandments apply, but waivers are available for seriously oppressed groups. An eleventh commandment has been added: "Thou shalt not speak ill of the disadvantaged," which has been reduced colloquially to "political correctness" and which Shelby Steele finds "redemptive."(26) Some commandments seem negotiable: burning and rioting are generally discouraged, but if the arsonists are descendants of slaves, not much punishment is required. As the Baltimore mayor opined in 2015 with regard to the riots in her city, "We give space to those who wish to destroy" Some sins may be overlooked if the transgressor is a fervent leftist. One may, for example, covet his neighbor's wife, even have sex with her, if he happens to be a member of the leftist elite or highly placed in the Democratic Party. Lenin's and Stalin's murders were committed on behalf of Socialism and therefore required no punishment. Mass murder for collective purposes, after all, can't be that bad.

Dennis Prager has written about the religious aspects of leftism.(27) Its adherents display their commitment to the disadvantaged proudly and often, signaling virtue even in casual conversation. Redemption will require improving the socioeconomic status of those defined by the Left as disadvantaged. "Social injustice" must be destroyed wherever it is found, and the crusade leading to utopia has been proclaimed. Since humor is the beginning of heresy, ethnic humor, which once eased life in multiethnic America, is banned. Expiation for historical sinning requires a restrictive speech. The disciples of leftism include our liberal community neighbors, and the violence of recent leftist "antifascist" (antifa) attacks on the political Right express the fervor of this quasi-religious movement. Von Mises noted a religious quality in Marx:

> 'He preaches a doctrine of salvation which rationalizes peoples' resentment (of the wealthy) and trans-figures their envy and desire for revenge into a mission ordained by world history. He inspires them with a consciousness of their mission by greeting them as those who carry in themselves the future of the human race. The rapid expansion of Socialism has been compared to that of Christianity. More appropriate, perhaps, would be a comparison with Islam, which inspired to lay waste of ancient civilizations.' (3)

Marxist demagoguery has combined with the rhetoric of the racial industry to become the Left's specialty. America's inequities have become "social injustice", wrought not just by greedy capitalists, but by bigoted white men. Those falling well to the Left on the bell curve are "the disadvantaged." Economic underperformance can't be explained by disparities in group abilities, we are told. Rather, low earners are victims of bigotry, discrimination, and white supremacy. Attempts to explain poverty as due to anti-intellectualism, poor personal discipline, and a criminal subculture are met with accusations of racism. With a religious zeal long absent in the United States, devoted leftists are undermining America's faith in itself, destroying its founding myths, and insisting that the US Constitution was improperly conceived by greedy and hypocritical men. Our history is reinterpreted and deconstructed. This revisionist view says that the European discoveries of the New World brought only disease and rapine to the native 'noble savage' of America.

> Columbus himself has been deconstructed by the Left, even '...though not a single new fact about Columbus' life and exploits had been uncovered, and America's mood swung from one of uncritical adulation to one of loathing and condemnation, at least among members of the "intellectual" class. The change was accomplished by the aggressive ideology of multiculturalism. The Columbus turnaround is merely a specific instance of more general alterations in our moral landscape.' (20)

As America's founding wickedness is increasingly understood, it supports Mr. Obama's contention that "fundamental transformation" is required. A greedy, exclusionary, imperialistic, and war-mongering nation will, under socialism, become egalitarian, redistributive, inclusive, altruistic, and peace-loving. It will, in other words, follow the prescriptive advice of liberal-leftism and provide not just material wealth but a collective sense of moral purpose, which capitalism's individuality has been unable to furnish:

> 'Western states do provide good social services, economic opportunity, and consumer goods, but they are increasingly indifferent to questions of meaning, to principles worth living, and perhaps dying, for ... A state that enshrines individual freedom must allow citizens to pursue their private ideas of the good, as the state itself is barred from laying claim on transcendent values. Liberalism replaces arguments over the most efficient means for achieving material ends. ... The Trump presidency and the EU crisis ... point to a yearning for a political approach to life's fundamental questions.' (22)

IX

Black America, the Racism Racket, and Affirmative Action:

'Senator Joseph McCarthy's infamous question was: Are you now or have you ever been a communist? If he were now to be suddenly resurrected, surely his first question would be: 'Are you now or have you ever been a racist?'
RM

Wax said that bourgeois norms were needed: "Get married before you have children, and strive to stay married for their sake. Get the education you need for gainful employment, work hard, and avoid idlenessEschew substance abuse and crime" (101)

'…sympathy for the negro and the poor goes hand in hand with an elitist conceit that pits intellectuals against the egalitarian masses. They will fight for the negro and the poor, but they have no use for the common folk who work and moonlight to take care of their own.' (18)

Black America forms about 15 percent of the population. While some blacks have advanced socioeconomically and a few have become intellectual and economic leaders, many remainwho seem unable to rise above ghetto life; some of them have adopted a criminal subculture, and a small number of African-Americans are responsible for most murders in the United States (80, 86) Leftist dogma will explain this subculture as a response to white bigotry, but Sowell sees it differently:

'Any serious study of racial and ethnic groups…repeatedly encounters…large and numerous disparities among these groups, whether in income, education, crime rates, IQs, or many other things… Sometimes minorities are on the short end of disparities (as in US, UK, and France), sometimes…the majority….Sometimes the disparities are blamed on discrimination, sometimes on genes, but in any event the disparities are treated as oddities that need explaining, (no matter how common such supposed

oddities are in countries around the world)...Where minorities have outperformed politically dominant majorities...it is difficult to make the case that discrimination is the cause...But a more fundamental question must be faced: was there ever any realistic chance that the various races would have had the same skills, experience, and general capabilities, even if they had the same genetic potential and faced no discrimination?' (35)

To be sure, the white underclass described by Vance and Murray (102,103) is in many ways as disadvantaged as blacks, but blacks have been chosen by the left as poster-children for America's indelible 'otherism'. And, as Glaser points out (80), even northern blacks, who were spared much of Southern Jim Crow segregation, are nonetheless included in the ever-larger leftist army of victims. Blacks have been persuaded that (a) their great-grandfathers were the only slaves the world has ever known, and (b) history has never seen such bigotry as they encounter daily. The educational rigor required to educate them for capitalism is perceived by many as further white oppression, and they insist that we have skimped on their educational funding. The importance of cultural group disparities in ability, as described by Thomas Sowell, is denied, and the left insists that black underachievement must be the result of white bigotry. The great expansion of the US welfare state seems to have occurred as The Great Society and The War on Poverty began, about 1965. While not eliminating ghettoes, these have been vote-buying programs par excellence. Jason Riley describes their adverse effects:

'Between 1890 and 1940, black marriage rates in the United States were higher than white ... black labor participation rates exceeded those of whites; black incomes grew much faster than white, ... and the black poverty rate fell. Between 1940 and 1970, ... during Jim Crow and prior to affirmative action, the number of blacks in middle-class professions quadrupled. In other words, racial gaps were narrowing...(but) in the post-60s era, these positive trends would slow, stall ... or reverse ... The homicide rate rose by nearly '90%' Disadvantaged groups have been hit hardest by the disintegration of ... middle-class mores, and ... the expansion of the welfare state, which reduced the financial need for two-parent families, hastened social retrogression The number of single parents grew astronomically, producing children more prone to academic failure, addiction, idleness, crime, and poverty.' (100)

Since the white majority is seen by the liberal Left as the cause of African-American dysfunction, whites need to atone by alleviating their povertyHence, the many welfare programs adopted by state and central governments that subsidize food, housing, and other daily needs. In addition, affirmative action is hoped to redress the educational deficit in minority communities. More recently, financial reparation for slavery has been proposed, either in cash or, as a few black legislators have urged, transferring title of white-owned houses to poor blacks. Prolonged government charity has produced a subculture without work ethic or fathers, which prizes violence and breeds anti-intellectualism.

Attempts to establish an eight-hour- day-five-day-week work ethic are perceived by many black leaders as further white oppression. Drugs are ubiquitous.

Federal and State handouts have continued since the mid-1960s, perhaps in part because their sudden withdrawal might provoke civil unrest and probably also because the left prefers poor constituents and their votes. Political patronage enables ghetto leaders to improve their personal finances while providing little for their constituents but sympathy. The racism industry, in particular, is at pains to remind African Americans of their historical and ongoing 'oppression' and encourages self-pity by insisting that whites have rigged the commercial game, and contrive to hold them back. Convinced that they cannot succeed, many do not. And, even when well-meaning, charity continues to destroy minority communities. Hear Charles Murray: 'If we were to... give every family enough money to put them above poverty line...two things would happen. First, the number of families(asking for help)...would increase. Second, the suffering in inner cities would go on..."(53)

Is it true that black disadvantage in America is due to white bigotry? If that's so, how do we explain that African-born immigrants to the United States regularly outperform native blacks? Naomi Riley describes a ...'remarkable' roll call of high-flying immigrant African-American students who were accepted into all eight ivy-league universities." She asks:

'Why does racism not seem to keep black immigrants down? The answer is obvious: black immigrant culture tends to value academic achievement and believes it is possible to excel no matter what happened to your ancestors ... If you start thinking ... that the whole system is against us, then you cannot succeed. American-born black groups like the Cornell Black Student Union insist that the system is out to get them and they cannot succeed. That makes the presence of high-achieving black students inconvenient, and they call on the university to disfavor immigrants, ... citing the African Holocaust in America ... and urging greater affirmative action for native blacks.' (56)

'...Black Americans, we hoped, might adopt the values that contributed to better white academic and economic performance. But adopting them is seen by some as a denial of the validity of black culture, and whites who urge bourgeois values are seen as oppressors, reminding of slave-owner tyranny. The importance of those values (delayed marriage, job skills, responsibility for progeny) is denied by the Left, who believe that African-Americans have created a unique culture which should be encouraged in its separateness; as multiculturalism insists, all cultures are equally valid. But it seems increasingly clear that all cultures are not equally productive of valuable citizens. In fact, those cultures which encourage self-restraint, delayed gratification, marriage, and a strong work ethic tend to thrive. Those that tolerate or excuse substance abuse, out-of-wedlock pregnancy, and dropping out tend to break down" (101).

These insights are denied by Angry academics who police the prevailing narrative of black victimhood. According to this narrative, black progress is determined not by personal choices and individual behavior but by white supremacy, America's history of slavery and discrimination, and institutional racism; touting "bourgeois values" is interpreted as an offense against authentic black culture. But'... so-called bourgeois values have always empowered (blacks)to persevere and overcome bitter oppression. They provided the glue that held the black community together during the hardest of times. (ibid)

What Woodson calls the 'prevailing narrative' of black victimhood and oppression has been enthusiastically adopted and propagated by America's racism industry and the political Left. The Reverends Jackson and Sharpton make a good living convincing blacks that white people hate, exploit, and subjugate them and are responsible for black economic underachievement:

'Al Sharpton clones, if not the man himself, (are) ready to spin the tale of black tragedy and white bigotry. Such people, and the American left generally, have a hunger for racism that is almost cravenThe sweetness at the core of hard news, say the death of ... a young black man is that ... not all is lost;it looks like racism.(Even though) today Americans know that active racism is no longer the greatest barrier to minority achievement ... and that white racism didn't shoot more than four thousand people last year in Chicago, ... the Left can't let racism go as one of its major causes. If bigotry is pronounced dead, the racket is over.' (105)

Leftism thrives on this ethnic and social division, and encourages it, seeing it as a path to instability and a soft socialist revolution. The narrative that high black incarceration rates reflect racism continues, even though, as Heather MacDonald has shown, black incarceration rates reflect a higher propensity for crime, which Goldberg affirms: "The reality is that 6 percent of the American people are black males and commit half of American murders" (80).

America's compassion seems to have raised crime rates and illegitimacy, especially among minorities. In 1960, the number of crimes per 100,000 population was 1887; by 1969, there were 3680, and by 1980 5950.(106). Combined illegitimacy (white and black) was 5 percent in 1960 but 30 percent in 1991; among blacks, it had risen to 68 percent. In 2017, the University of Illinois said that 85 percent of Chicago's black teens were out of work. During the 2017 July 4 weekend, Chicago had sixty-four shootings and eight deaths, all in the black community(104) Since 2011, there have been 19,000 shootings in Chicago, and over 4000 murders; the average number of murders peryear is 541,mostly in the black community. 71% of Chicago's murders are committed by blacks(107) Despite these numbers, liberals insist that black incarceration rates are high because of racist police, who target blacks for surveillance, arrest, and imprisonment. If black men are surveilled closely, it is not because of bigoted police (many of whom are black), but because that's where crime is likely to occur. When the left blames high incarceration on bigotry, the black community is absolved of its need to reduce criminal behavior, and explains its violence on prolonged white discrimination. Some police officers now avoid policing black neighborhoods, fearing (a) violent criminals, (b) accusations of racism if arrests are required, and (c) indictment and prosecution if 'political correctness' is violated, followed by (d) career and pension loss. 'Broken Windows' policing provided a more intense surveillance of street criminals in NewYork City, and successfully reduced violent crime. But the Left opposes it, on grounds of 'racial profiling', and has discouraged its continuation; without it, ghetto communities may become even more crime-ridden, since poor black citizens are often the victims of black crime. (Responding to complaints of unnecessary roughness by police, some satirical wags have called for "genteel policing," which would exclude unpleasant physical confrontation between perpetrators and police: pleasant greetings, formal introductions and hand-shaking would be followed by elaborate ingratiation by the officers.)

Ferguson Missouri is near St. Louis. Michael Brown, an African-American shoplifter, was arrested in that suburb after extorting items from a small store. Rather than surrendering, he reached for the arresting officer's pistol and was shot and killed. Leftist media, local and national, misrepresented this event and claimed that Mr. Brown was killed while surrendering, despite video to the contrary. Many in the black community insisted that Brown's death was due to racist policing, and a protest group calling themselves Black Lives Matter' (BLM) was formed, whose marches urged assassination of police officers ("pigs in a blanket"). This group was further animated when Freddy Gray, a small-time hood and drug-dealer in Baltimore, died following arrest and transport in a police vehicle, perhaps due to self-inflicted injury. Rioting and looting in Baltimore followed his death, where the mayor famously remarked that rampage "was needed to decompress" a black community long oppressed by whites. The officers involved in Gray's arrest, black and white, were subsequently prosecuted on charges of murder; recently all were acquitted, but potential police recruits must now be aware of the media's tendency to distort police encounters with black perpetrators and the legal complications arising therefrom.

Baltimore's mayor is not alone:

'...rage is common to all ghetto blacks'says Alvin Francis Poussaint (35) During the Los Angeles riots, for example,

> 'The people of Watts felt that for those four days of rioting, they represented all negroes; the historic plight of the negroes; all the rebellions against all injustice ... What must be understood by the rest of America is that, for the lower-class negro, riots are not criminal but a legitimate weapon in a morally justified civil war.'(105)

There are those, then, who justify the rioting in Watts, Detroit, and elsewhere. But the effect of the rioting was detrimental, most of all to the black communities themselves, and it was rioting that led to poverty, not the reverse. Further, the motives for rioting are not simply emotional 'decompression':

'They riot for criminal reasons like looting and because mob action seems to be taking on the action of a fad. Bedeviled the police, strip stores, shout and yell, crush anyone who opposes you … and if the police try to stop it, just yell "brutality." … Arson and looting in the guise of protest is a form of self-sabotage.' 106

Black Lives Matter (BLM) is seen by the left as an opportune movement, which, if properly financed and favored by liberal media, has great potential for dividing and subverting America. It feeds the post-slavery exclusionary narrative in which white-supremacist bigots hate and discriminate against blacks, perpetuate Jim Crow, and prevent black achievement. This narrative absolves blacks of personal responsibility for their underachievement and convinces that their economic failure is inevitable, and America's poor are doomed to remain so until wealth is redistributed. So BLM has become another arrow in the liberal-leftist-socialist quiver.

Anxious to display sympathy for, and lobby on behalf of, these 'damaged' groups, the Democrats are now referred to as the "Pity Party." Perpetually aggrieved, they say violent black disorder is due to ostracism by whites and that 'something must be done' But pandering prevents leftist politicians from speaking truth to their constituents. Mr. Obama could have averted several police assassinations by denouncing BLM publicly, but an election was approaching, and any criticism of that bloc would have been untimely. Declining to denounce BLM and its brazen civil disorder, the president implicitly endorsed its behavior. The man whose two-term presidency demonstrated America's commitment to undo racism could have unified us, but instead pandered for a few more votes and encouraged further racial division. Obama, whose very career denied significant racism in the United States, could have calmed several racially-charged situations during his terms, but instead chose to endorse black civil disorder by tacitly agreeing with its appropriateness. Instead of denouncing disruption of the public peace, his unspoken agreement with it reminds us of his leftism.

One of medical school's most useful messages is *primum non nocere*: first, do no harm: When confronting disease, the young physician is warned to avoid the adverse effects of intervening too hastily. Leftists ignore that lesson, perhaps because their social policies, even when failing, hasten the demise of America's capitalist order; they will answer failure by asking for more time and money. One of their policies subsidized young single mothers, as long as fathers were absent. Hear Judge Bork:

'It is madness to offer an apartment of her own and a steady income to an unmarried young woman or girl if she will only have…another… baby while remaining unmarried. As she has additional children, her income rises. The availability of welfare relieves the father of any responsibility that he might have felt.'(20)

Again: 'The presence of a decent father helps a male child control aggression; his absence impedes it … when the (unwed) mother is also a teenager…in urban America, the consequences for the child are even grimmer … The children suffer cognitive defects … and display … poorly controlled aggression.' (ibid 2003)

So violence in these subsidized neighborhoods increases in direct proportion to paternal absence. 'The evidence is now overwhelming that the collapse of marriage is creating a whole generation of children less happy, less equipped to deal with life … or work, and more dangerous to themselves and others (ibid These are the effects of 50 years of liberal social policy and vote-buying, and they won't be easy to undo; withdrawing food stamps and cash infusions from those who have known only handouts for several generations might be the beginning of civil war.

'An obvious'… effort… then, is the drastic restructuring of welfare. That will be difficult for several reasons. For one, there is a major constituency opposed to any change … other than an increase in welfare benefits. This constituency is made up not just of welfare recipients; its most vociferous component is modern liberals of the welfare-is-a-right-not-a-privilege persuasion. The left wing of the Democratic Party finds it profitable to resist any welfare reform on the stated ground that they are protecting children from Republican rapacity that would have those children sleeping on the grates.'   (ibid p 160)

'The most common argument for affirmative action in higher education is that it provides a "remedy" for … past racial discrimination. … [But] … it is not possible to remedy an injury to A caused by B by giving a benefit to C at the expense of D.' (75)

"The only legitimiacy for affirmative action was to make up for the fact that they were enslaved, or…treated as enslaved…thereafter. We never made it up, and there is no way of making it up'(80)

The idea that historical injury can be repaired is a bit absurd. The notion that slavery can now be remedied is especially so, since neither slaves nor slaveholders have been seen in America for 150 years. Nevertheless, the Left and some radical black groups continue to urge recompense for past oppression. Ignoring the law, which defines a statute of limitations, the left asks for undefined financial (or other) compensation as expiation for our historical sins. But reparations sometimes lead to further conflict. After WWI, France insisted reparations be paid to them by Germany; unable to pay in specie, the Weimar Republic printed enormous amounts of paper money, which finally bankrupted Germany and became a major factor causing WWII. Nonetheless, the Left insists that some compensation be made to African-Americans for slavery, Jim Crow, and alleged ongoing discrimination. White oppression must somehow be expiated. Limited intellectual achievement, they say, has been the result of bigotry and underinvestment in black schooling. These factors, according to the left, account for continued ghettoism and must somehow be repaired.

Affirmative action is one liberal solution to 'white supremacy' and an attempt to atone for "white privilege" in America. Many on the left recommended lowering of requirements for admission to US colleges and graduate schools, believing that these requirements are simply another way to unfairly exclude blacks from higher education. Lowering requirements for more than fifty years has resulted in many blacks attending and some graduating. But instead of properly matching black intellectual ability to appropriate schools, and despite knowing that most blacks, once admitted, underperform whitesthere has been an effort to admit them to elite schools, often a mismatch, where their underperformance has led to self-doubt, dropping out, and a low graduation rate. Further, those who do graduate often feel that they have been advanced improperly, and that their white counterparts hold their degrees in contempt. And while many on the Left congratulate themselves for affirmative action, they are ignoring the detrimental effects of these programs on some poorly prepared minority students.

'...the average black 12th grader performs at the level of the average white 8th grader in reading and math. Reflecting this four-year deficiency, the average black college applicant scores about 200 points lower than the average white or Asian on the SAT. Rather than addressing this basic problem, racially preferential admissions programs pretend that it doesn't exist. Further, the gap has actually increased in the past ten years...' (75)

Instead of advancing black students socioeconomically, affirmative action has, in many respects, reaffirmed their sense of inadequacy:

'The effect of race preference is...to place them in a school more selective than a school for which they are fully qualified and would otherwise have attended—the mismatch effect. (They)...are thus placed at an academic disadvantage, and typically a large one...Blacks do better academically...and (have better)) bar passage rates in schools for which they are fully competitive...'(ibid)

Affirmative Action is social-engineering with a decidedly mixed outcome. it excludes non-black, often better-prepared students from admission and violates one basic American principle: that discrimination must not exist on the basis of skin color. For those excluded, it is reverse discrimination. Why does the Left believe that it can squeeze underprepared applicants into positions where they are forced to compete against those better prepared? And why should they believe that an anti-intellectual black subculture can be overridden by their insistence that all cultures are equal? If children are not properly educated in primary school systems, why would we think that simply pushing them forward by lowering standards will lead to success? Many poor whites also underperform in school, and we don't usually recommend mismatching them at the college level. But the sense of white guilt surrounding black underperformance persuades many leftists that something expiatory must be done, and the underprepared black child becomes a guinea pig for overcompassionate leftists, who will insist that they "meant well" when affirmative action fails.

It is politically incorrect to say, or even think, that black culture spurns learning,. but it is largely true, and where anti-intellectualism prevails, the intervention of the left is likely to have little beneficial effect on black performance. Again, Lino Graglia, willing to speak the unspeakable:

'The whole point of … racial preference programs is to evade and camouflage the fact that the groups preferred by the programs cannot otherwise compete with others for admission to selective institutions of higher education…. In general, more than half of the students in the bottom 10 percent of a school's IQ range will be black.' (Ibid)

Despite evidence that affirmative action, far from elevating minority students, in fact harms them, the left insists that these programs must continue. They insist that enough time and money hasn't yet been invested. But there is a larger issue as well, especially whem it becomes clear that academic standards are being lowered to ease minority performance.

'No community can be built on the basis of preferential treatment and double standards, and their existence belies university rhetoric about equality. Conflicting standards of excellence and justice are the root of the bitter and divisive controversies over admissions, curricular content, and race relations on campus….the university administration is responsible for betraying student idealism and replacing it with cynicism and resentment…' (12)

For some minority students, activism replaces classroom excellence, and instead of learning, four years are devoted to proclaiming their victimhood, segregating themselves in black fraternities from which whites are excluded, and organizing protests to force concessions from an apparently intimidated college administration. A few black students who wish to assimilate and associate with white student groups are ostracized by other blacks.

College and university administrators seem unwilling or unable to reestablish discipline in the many cases where students, invading campus buildings, insist on preferential treatment and protection from unpleasant lectures which recount past oppression. This apparent inability may hide a larger truth: the American insistence on the baccalaureate as a badge of entry into the middle class has created unprecedented opportunity for college treasuries, and nobody wants to rock the fiscal boat:

'American colleges and universities were once little more than finishing schools for the wealthy. At the end of the Civil War, there were only 112,000 undergraduate students in the US…A century and a half later, the Education Department estimates the student population at 20 million, and the bachelor's degree is regarded as the middle class's key of promise...' (76)

Upon realizing this enormous potential benefit to academe's bottom line, administrators seem to have agreed that, while discipline and academic achievement on campus may have to be eased a bit in order to accommodate these larger and less capable student-bodies, the resulting fiscal advantages will far outweigh the intellectual corner-cutting. Further, many faculty members are hostile to the capitalist order, as Schumpeter predicted, and may indeed encourage campus anarchy.

Politics, money, and subversion have created chaos at many colleges. Affirmative action has failed for unprepared black students, and has made some campuses a source of strong anti-American sentiment. Instead of assimilaton, racial division is strengthened, and animus towards minority students by those rejected for admission is created. Racial affirmative action should be abandoned, replaced by preferential treatment for those willing to demonstrate their commitment and talent for learning, especially when held back by socioeconomic limitations. Students of all colors should be chosen on the basis of:
'...factors such as family background, financial condition, and ...school environment, giving preference...as long as it is clear that these students can be reasonably expected to meet the academic challenges of the selective college. Race or ethnicity, however, would cease to count either for or against any applicant.' (12)

X

The Homosexual Lobby, LGBTQ, and Leftism

- California, where I live, now offers birth certificates with a third option, neither boy nor girl. they call it nonbinary.' (AdeCarlo, WSJ)

The leftist Democratic Party, to review, has collected a series of marginalized, disadvantaged groups as voting blocs. Their intent is to ameliorate these groups socially, to 'normalize' them, lift their "oppression," and to erase the bigotry that allegedly surrounds and 'disadvantages' them. In defense of homosexuals, the Left insists that they have been marginalized by a vague biblical proscription and that their historic ostracism is simply "otherness"; when fully understood, says the Left, the homosexual lifestyle will be seen as wholesome as the straight. Those who denounce their way of life are simply arrogant, stupid traditionalists, "deplorables" with guns and Bibles. Hollywood in particular has assisted in "normalizing" homosexuality, and many of its productions insist on presenting increasingly graphic and gratuitous sex between males. At firstthese scenes were shadowed and therefore less explicit; (e.g., *Brokeback Mountain*); recently, however we have been presented with nude males preparing for anal sex (e.g., *The Assassination of Gianni Versace*). Offensive to some perhaps, but Hollywood considers these scenes as important in fulfilling its leftist agenda. The homosexual lobby is, after all, vocal and well financed.

Historically, homosexuals have been ostracized because of the high incidence of disease that their lifestyle encourages, and this may explain the biblical proscription. Anal sex promotes syphilis, gonorrhea, herpes simplex, amebiasis, Epstein-Barr, giardiasis. Hepatitis, colitis, enteritis, and proctitis occur at high rates among homosexual men. Anal disease is common, especially cancer. In recent years, AIDS, which destroys immunity to major disease, has been epidemic, usually carried by homosexuals and drug addicts. Tuberculosis, largely eliminated in the United States, has been resurrected by AIDS.

- 'Tuberculosis has been controlled mainly in Europe and the US In the last part of the twentieth century because of social improvements, better health conditions ... and ... developments in antibiotics. ... We thought we had things controlled ..., but ... with the rise of AIDS, we are entering an alarming epidemic situation. In the new millennium, nearly 2 billion people—onethird of the world's population—are infected with the bacterium that causes tuberculosis. ... One could estimate that 100 to 200 million people might develop active TB during their lifetimesDeveloping active TB is very much related to the (human) immune system. Once a person develops AIDS, the chances (of active TB) become rampant...' (108)

Many AIDS victims, notably from Haiti, were encouraged to migrate to America by the "compassionate" Left, who ignored the inevitable infection among drug addicts and homosexuals which would result. The resurgence of TB among homosexuals and drug-users (homosexuals are especially likely to use drugs while having sex) was predictable, but, ignored in the name of sympathy for Haitians.

'National officials identified Haitians as a health threat in the 1970s. TB was allegedly endemic among them ... In the 1980s, the Center for Disease Control identified them as one of the primary groups at risk for AIDS. ... The Food and Drug Administration in the 1980s refused to accept blood donated by Haitians ... for fear of AIDS contamination']. (Amnesty International, internet)

The spread of AIDS would have been much better controlled if (a) anal sex had been abandoned, (b) promiscuity among homosexuals had diminished, as advised, and (c) drug use had not been so common during homosexual encounters. Instead, these precautions seem to have been largely ignored. Despite this unwillingness to protect themselves and the larger US population, LGBT has been enthusiastically normalized, even made to seem heroic, by the political Left. Ostracism, originally because of disease, has undergone leftist revision, and is now blamed on the political right; white supremacists discouraged Haitian immigration because of black skin. Opposing the arrival of diseased black men confirms your bigotry and homophobia.

Pandering to the Lesbian, Gay, Bisexual and Transgender lobbies by leftist Democrats now knows no limits. The absurdity grows, and children are encouraged at an early age to think beyond genitalia, and describe their genders according to emotional proclivity. A few physicians are ready to assist in changing gender with the appropriate hormones, and sympathetic bureaucrats have proposed eliminating 'biological gender' on birth certificates, to be replaced by 'sex assigned at birth'. This is intended to ease the child's (apparently arbitrary) decision as to its gender, regardless of genital identity. Further, compassionate academics have devised new terms for the 'fluid gendered':

Transgenders now insist on being referred to as '...ze, sie, hir, co, ev, xe...(or)...thon,...and California threatens to jail health workers who refuse to use ...(these new)...pronouns', ... (in New York)...'business owners who intentionally use the wrong pronoun with transgender workers and tenants face potential fines of as much as $250,000...If there is any issue that can rouse conservatives and drive them to the polls, it is this one...if gender activists prevail,...(conservatives)...will be left with a world they neither recognize nor like very much...'(110)

In Charlotte, city officials decided that bathroom use should be decided by the stated gender of the user. The fluidity of gender, then, would replace the long-established custom of segregating the sexes in bathrooms, and gender could be defined only by him/her (ze, sie, xe?). Traditionals were disturbed by this new policy, fearing some young males would declare themselves temporarily transgender just for a peek in the girls' stalls. But the left insisted that young transgenders were confused and menaced by the presence of isosexuals. North Carolina briefly threatened to limit restroom use according to genital gender, but, under pressure from the LGBTQ lobby, relented. The absurdity of the issue defines how far the left will strain credulity to comfort its base.

Conclusion

'Can Capitalism Survive? No, I do not think it can.' Schumpeter, J (8)

Schumpeter thought that socialism in the United States is inevitable. He may be right. There are several factors which make America vulnerable to radical political change, including:

I: Ignorance, bibliophobia
II: Unstable poor and minority communities
III: Immigration, legal and illegal: Importing the enemy
IV: Inequality of material wealth, redistribution, and the risk of bankruptcy

I: AMERICA the IGNORANT

'Nobody ever went broke underestimating the intelligence of the American public.'
H.L. Mencken

Alex Berezow: quotes his Polish wife about the incompetence of the US school system: the best-liked students were also the smartest in Poland, but not in the United States, where athletes and cheerleaders were most popular...

'...getting rid of that (aristocratic) tradition (will be like) the extraction of an essential organ without which it can no longer healthily survive...as divisive and anarchic in its consequences as...France's liquidation of its aristocracy in 1789, from which she did not recover... until Charles deGaulle...' (115)

'There is a cult of ignorance in the United States, and there always has been. The strain of anti-intellectualism has been a constant thread winding its way through our political and cultural life, nurtured by the false notion that democracy means that my ignorance is just as good as your knowledge' (116)

'Seventy-one percent of Americans can't identify the Constiturion as the supreme law of the land...Ten percent of college graduates think Judith Sheindlin (aka 'Judge Judy') sits on the Supreme Court...Only 32% can name all three branches of government, and 33% can't name a single one.'(117)

'A popular government, without popular information, is but a prologue to a farce or a tragedy, or perhaps both.' Franklin B. (117)

One advantage of having a privileged social class, whether we call them nobles, patricians, or aristocrats, is that their wealth and leisure permit them to pursue higher education and intellectual excellence. Britain's aristocracy has provided leadership and a paradigm for lesser classes for centuries. Unfortunately, America seems to have rejected aristocracy at the same time it renounced monarchy, and replaced it with antiintellectualism. It is understandable that book-learning might not be prized by frontiersmen, who need practical skills, but somehow formal learning came to be looked upon with disdain, perhaps because it suggested hierarchy and the upper- classism that America was repudiating. Ignorance was tolerated, even admired, and 'bookishness' became a pejorative. Even some presidents flaunted their ignorance: Lyndon Johnson's wife famously reported that LBJ didn't read books, but men. A radio show in the 1940s titled 'It Pays To Be Ignorant' satirized America's illiteracy, and found it amusing, but contempt for learning has created many intellectually vulnerable citizens. They hear leftist promises of wealth-sharing, free housing, education, medical care, and a guaranteed income, and begin to think that government has an unending supply of money which needs only to be properly apportioned for all to live happily under socialism. Ignorance accepts these promises without calculating costs and doesn't want to understand that collectivism ends badly. As we watch the left's dissolution of America's democratic- capitalist order, it is clear that a major cause is widespread ignorance. George W Bush reminded us of our bibliophobia at a press dinner attended by William F. Buckley: 'Mr Buckley, when you were at Yale, you wrote a book; when I was there I read one.'

Rather than learning, the US public school system creates a venue for daily socializing, where conversation ignores the daily lesson in favor of athletic and cheer-leader gossip. Intellectually-gifted students are often mocked, and the pretty girls prefer Mr. Touchdown. The order and educational rigor found, for example, in Catholic schools is absent in the public system, where one is more likely to encounter disorder, and the discipline enforced by nuns is often lacking. Mrs Berezow remarks that in Poland the best-liked students were also the smartest, and that schoolroom conversation often involved the latest learning; in the US, by contrast, students were most interested in who scored the latest touchdown, and the most admired were athletes and cheerleaders. Disdain for learning has always characterized parts of the US working class, often to the detriment of erudition. An excellent teacher's intent can easily be discouraged by parental apathy and scorn.

Classrooms, already disordered, became quasi-anarchic after integration, when black children seemed to see discipline as further white oppression, and often declined it. Then white children, feeling reverse discrimination by any attempt to keep order, also became unmanageable. Finally, under the current policy of political correctness, and the overused accusations of racism by the political left, any attempt to maintain order risks those accusations, as well as lawsuits by parents. The rhetoric about 'liberty' and 'freedom' is so often repeated and so generally misunderstood that it has come to mean the right to refuse discipline.

Some argue that reading by the US public was seriously damaged by radio, and then television. 24/7 entertainment leaves little time for genuine, useful learning. Many of our children are unprepared for the discipline required to master texts necessary for career education. Many have read nothing but the most popular and least-demanding fiction, and are overwhelmed in college. At the same time, the number of students aspiring to the baccalaureate, which has somehow become the key to the middle-class and beyond, has risen enormously and promises fiscal solvency for many academic institutions. Further, federal and state governments now augment and guarantee tuition payments. And so, keeping these young people as students becomes extremely important to administrators, even though academic standards must be lowered a bit, and even in the presence of violent political protestation among the student body.

America promises socioeconomic advancement as part of its national dream: my children will be wealthier and more admired than I am, goes the mantra. But poor academic performance limits upward mobility, especially in the poorest neighborhoods, and especially where ignorance prevails. It is the culture, then, which opposes a useful education, and even though ambitious politicians insist on higher taxes to spend more freely on education, more money isn't going to make much difference without a change in culture. Politicians promising advances in ghetto education can't help but see how antiintellectualism prevents improvement, but insist that higher taxes to 'invest in our children' will solve the problem. The results remain discouraging. Some groups will not learn well enough to succeed in capitalism, partly perhaps because of an anti-intellectual culture. And pretending that the problem can be solved by politicians will lead to ongoing failure.

'II: Unstable&Poor Communities'

Protesters at Aretha Franklin's funeral asked for 'more self-respect' from the white community, as if it could be handed out like welfare checks. But It can't. It is largely internal, learned in part at home. But the current practice of government funding for single mothers precludes a good home environment; further, it absolves the father of financial obligation and insists on his absence, which ensures aggressive and violent young black males. Hear Jasper Wiliams, a black Atlanta pastor:

'...the idea of children being raised without a provider father and a mother as nurturer is abortion after birth...in order to change America, we must change black America's culture. It must be done through parenting and in the home...black lives will not matter...until black people begin to respect their own lives. Once we begin to respect one another, then we can change... Anybody who thinks black America is all right as we are now is crazy. We're not allright...a lot of change needs to occur, and must come from within us...we have to change within ourselves. It is ludicrous for the church not to be involved. The church is the only viable institution we have in the African-American community. We must step up and turn our race around...' Winston-SalemJ (AP) 9/2/2018

America's poor African-American communities remain vulnerable to leftist subversion, which insists that they are victims of white oppression, and that their material underachievement is due to white cunning and a 'fixed game'. Their elected officials are increasingly explicit about how whites have 'disadvantaged' them and how physical confrontation might be used to right these terrible wrongs. In particular, a black Congresswoman woman representing Watts urges face-to-face hostility; her adherents have forced some government officials to leave their restaurant meals uneaten as they flee the harassment. This civil disorders could lead to serious violence, and the death of any black participant might spark a riot followed by calling out the National Guard; deaths among rioters or Guards might easily escalate and require further federal intervention. Depending on political and ethnic affiliations of the soldiers, the federal orders to quell the riots might or might not be obeyed, perhaps resulting in still more deaths and a developing and enlarging chaos. Shooting into the crowd often incites more tumult. Uncontrolled violence and murder might begin a civil war.

III: Immigration, Legal and Illegal: Importing the Enemy

Illegal immigrants in the US may number as many as 22-million. They have arrived showing disdain for our legal order, and, as Erler(1) suggests, contempt for our overactive compassion. Some illegals believe that the Southwestern United States is theirs by history, and, in a flagrant show of scorn, invert the American flag. Others fly the Mexican colors in its place. If serious separatism arises, one supposes it will be either in California (already calling for secession) or the other southwestern states bordering Mexico.

Islamic immigrants form a group inimical to our traditional religion and antithetical to our culture. In particular, because of their differing perception of the western female dress code, they are likely to offend by assaulting women, as on New Year's Eve in Germany, 2015. Their disdain for God and devotion to Allah encourage further violence, and in Scandinavia, they occupy separate but parallel communities which police avoid. Separatism rather than assimilation is their goal, and they are prone to murder with little provocation. To the extent that they prevent peaceful social order, they are instruments of turbulence and anarchy, and cause the unrest which might precipitate ungovernability and a leftist coup.

IV: Inequality of Material Wealth, Redistribution, and the Risk of Bankruptcy:

'A democracy is always temporary in nature...'(it lasts until)'... voters discover they can vote themselves generous gifts from the public treasury...' (then)...'the majority always votes for the candidates who promise the most benefits...with the result that every democracy collapses due to loose fiscal policy and is followed by dictatorship.'(38)

What is national bankruptcy like? We can all talk about hyperinflation and read about wheelbarrows of money in Weimar Germany, but what does it feel like to live it? We know that the price of Hemingway's coffee rose while he was drinking, which might be simply amusing unless one had budgeted at the early price. We've all heard that politicians in Venezuela printed so much valueless money that daily necessities like toilet–paper were unaffordable. But if the United States currency were to become worthless, be prepared to see everybody withdrawing money from their banks, all at the same time (bank runs); and be prepared to be the last guy in line, when the money runs out. Or maybe the bank will close just as you enter it, all accounts having been confiscated or frozen by the Federal Government. So without cash, and credit cards useless, prepare to feed yourself by rioting and looting at Kroger's or Food Lion. If you think this can't happen, know that it has occurred recently in Venezuela, Iceland, and Russia.

Referring to national bankruptcy, Niall Ferguson predicts a series of bank runs in Europe due to Greece's large debt. Many European countries, since the end of WWII, have flirted with bankruptcy due to enormous social welfare spending, in attempts to eliminate income disparity, and erase 'social injustice'. So, as the US seems intent on providing 'free' medical care for all, and subsidizes illegal immigrants to maybe $150 billion annually; and, while our nominal debt to China is about $20 trillion, and while Senator Sanders single-payer Medicare for all would cost $3.2 trillion annually, keep in mind that our national unfunded liabilities (Medicare, Medicaid, Social Security, etc) may exceed $150 trillion, (113). Watch the interest rates on US bonds: a sharp rise nearing 18-20% suggests that buyers suspect bankruptcy and are reluctant to buy unless very high rates justify the risk. Precipitous falls in stock prices sometimes predict bankruptcy. 'Social and political unrest can result'(111), and the left will be waiting for the anarchy which might precede a transition to socialism.

How might that transition occur? How will we know when capitalism is out and socialism in? In a period of great violence, military rule might precede a socialist coup; the military might support a despot in the name of restoring civil order. Historically, the despot has often arisen from the military. He might proclaim a socialist order and proceed to nationalize industry. But more likely, as the left continues to stress the 'injustice' of capitalist greed and its income disparity, there would be a peaceful transition to socialism, and an appropriate amendment would be added to our constitution(8). In that case, the left will have accomplished exactly what it intended.

POSTSCRIPT: Some conservatives are now calling for a Convention of States to amend the Constitution, hoping to prevent further encroachment by the left on its original meaning, and to instate congressional term limits. That sounds good, but how will the left's interference be prevented? Once the document is opened to change, what prevents the left from adding a socialist amendment, or eliminating free speech and the right to bear arms?

Bibliography

(1)Erler, E Imprimis 9/8/18, Hillsdale Coll.Hillsdale, MI

(2)RobertsonG1/16/18 WallStJJournal (WSJ)

(3)vonMisesL1981 SocialismLiberty Fund Indianapolis

(4)NoonanP12/24/17WSJ

(5)WisotskyM12/2/17 WSJ

(6)ServiceR2009 LeninMcMillan London

(7)MasonC1/7/18 WSJ

(8)SchumpeterJcAPITALISM, Socialism, and Democracy 1950 HarperNY

(9)KimballR1/30/18ltrsWSJ

(10)BrooksC Winston-Salem Journal, Winston-SalemNC (Corinne brooks)

(11)KennedyJF1/20/61InauguralAddress

(12)D'SouzaD1991FreePressNY

(13)RoveK8/16/18WSJ

(14)HusockH7/12/17CorpPubBrdcasting WSJ

(15)Will, G: Winston-SalemJ(NPR, PBS, CorpPubBroad)

(16)ContinettiM WSJ

(17)O'HareTWSJltrs 8/17/17

(18)HofferE NYTimes1970

(19)PolybiusTheHistories 2009OverlandParkDigireadsPublishing

(20)BorkRSlouching towards Gomorrah1996HarperCollins New York

(21)BrennerR2/26/17WSJ22)HenningerD12/7/17WSJ

(23)EpsteinJ6/2/17 WSJBkReview

(24)McGurnW11/7/17WSJ

(25)NeiburgerEJ11/11/17WSJ

(26)SteeleS8/28/17WSJ

(27)PragerDInternet

(28)RosenC10/23/17WklyStd

(29)BrzezinskiZ1989TheGrandFailureScribnersNY

(30)SchueckH Envy

(31)Weingarten11/11/17WSJ

(32)TrendelS11/11/17ImprimisHillsdaleCollMI

(33)DuddlestonK8/19/17WSJ

(34)TupiB8/19/17WSJ

(35)SowellTIntellectuals&Race2013PerseusBksPhila

(36)CoganJ9/5/18WSJ

(37)DelayK1/17/18WSJ

(38)TytlerAInternet

(39)NoonanP1/13/18WSJ

(40)SwaimB12/15/17WSJ

(41)MurrayDStrangeDeathofEurope2018BloomsburyLondon

(42)wishonW6/17/17WSJ

(43)SperryP3/10/18NYPost

(44)RossiRWSJ

(45)TraubJ7/5/17BkRev'Refuge'WSJ

(46)DalrympleJLifeatthe Bottom2001IvanDeeChicago

(47GreenD12/7/17WSJLtrs

(48)SnidermanPWhenWaysofLife Collide

(49)HazonyY10/14/17WSJ

(50)DalrympleT6/5/17TerrorWSJ

(51)WilsonJQCrime&HumanNature1985FreePressNewYork

(52)FriedmanMCapitalism&FreedomUnivChicagoPressChicago

(53)OlaskyVTragedyofAmericanCompassion1994RegneryWashington

(54)DelayK1/17/18WSJ

(55)FinleyJ1/8/18WSJ

(56)RileyNS10/18/17WSJ

(57)NoonanP1/13/18WSJ

(58)SwaimB12/15/17WSJ

(59)HaydnT1962PortHuronStatement

(60)NYTaskForceonMinorities198

(61)LammRPlantoDestroyAmerica2004WashingtonDC

(62)SperryP3/10/18NYPost

(63)Dailytelegraph1/3/18London(WSJ)

(64)RoyAWSJ1/3/18WSJ

(65)Finley9/25/17WSJ

(66)Obamacare'sDeathPayments11/23/17WSJ

(67)TyrellREFutureThatDoesn'tWork1977DoubledayNY

(68)CarterM1/11/17WSJ

(69)TezelliD11/1/17WSJ

(70)AtkinsB6/6/17WSJ

(71)WatsonO6/6/17WSJ

(72)RoveK8/6/18WSJ

(73)KaufmanS10/19/17WSJ

(74)ThomasCTheDoctorisNotIn8/23/18Winston-SalemJ

(75)GragliaLAffirmativeActionFraud InterNet

(76)GuelzoA8/25-26/18WSJ

(77)GossPWSJ

(78)GoldbergSFads&FallaciesinSocSci2003HumanityBooksAmherstNY

(79)KesslerAConfirmationBias&Pseudoscience8/14/17WSJ

(80)GlazerNEthnicDilemmas9/15-16WSJ

(81)HillAB(UKStatistician)EmpiricismInternet

(82)KristolW9/4/17WklyStdeditorial

(83)ThomasCStarvingtheGovernmentBeast12/6/17Opinion

(84)Liemetal1/16/14JinterpersonalViolence

(85)MorseS&SatelS10/1/17WSJ

(86)MacDonaldH10/10/17WSJ

(87)SaltermanM11/25/17WSJ

(88)LakeA11/17Winston-SalemJ

(89)deCarloAR1/2/18WSJ

(90)RobertsonG1/16/18WSJ

(91)WatsonPJSexodus12/14/14WSJ

(92)HistoryofFeminismInternet

(93)BritishHistoryofFeminismPlatoShrugsInternet

(94)QuilletteFeminismBlindsstudentstotruthAboutMen

(95)TarantoJ9/23/17WSJ

(96)MillerJ6/21/17WSJ

(97)Waxinyourears9/21/17ltrsWSJ

(98)EberstadtMPrimalScream11/6/17WklyStd

(99)WillickJIdentityPoliticsBkReview12/15/17WSJ

(100)RileyJ4/12/18Newsweek

(101)WoodsonR10/11/17WSJ

(102)VanceJDHillbillyElegy2016HarperCollinsNY

(103)MurrayCComingApart2012RandomHouseNY

(104)SteeleS8/28/17WSJ

(105)HardCoreGhettoMood8/21/67Newsweek

(106)HusockHRiots, LootingWSJ

(107)MorrowL9/18/18WSJ

(108)RoscignoG2001AventisSAInternet

(109)AmnestyInternationalInternet

(110)ShrierA8/30/18WSJ

(111)HallS7/26/17Bizfluent

(112)FergusonN7/26/17Bizfluent

(113)FoxxVirginiaPersonalCommunication

(114)BerizonAInternet

(115)WorsthornePInDefenseofArostocracy2004HarperCollinsLondon

(116)AsimovI1/21/80Newsweek

(117)WillettD9/17/18WSJ

CPSIA information can be obtained
at www.ICGtesting.com
Printed in the USA
BVHW071435260819
556808BV00015B/863/P